DATE DUE

A Promise in Haiti

A Promise in Haiti

*A Reporter's Notes
on Families and Daily Lives*

Mark Curnutte

*Foreword by Kenneth H. Merten,
U.S. Ambassador to Haiti*

With photographs by the author

Vanderbilt University Press
Nashville

© 2011 by Vanderbilt University Press
Nashville, Tennessee 37235
All rights reserved
First printing 2011

Brief passages from "Introduction: Dinner Hour" and
"Afterword: Under the Mango Tree" have appeared
in the *Cincinnati Enquirer* and are reprinted by
permission.

Library of Congress Cataloging-in-Publication Data

Curnutte, Mark.
A promise in Haiti : a reporter's notes on families and
daily lives / Mark Curnutte ; foreword by Kenneth H.
Merten, with photographs by the author.
p. cm.
Includes bibliographical references and index.
ISBN 978-0-8265-1783-8 (cloth edition : alk. paper)
1. Poor—Haiti—Gonaïves. 2. Disasters—Haiti—
Gonaïves. I. Title.
HC153.Z7G66 2011
972.9407'3—dc22
2010047264

In Memoriam
Elizabeth A. Curnutte
(1929–2006)
John T. Curnutte
(1923–2003)

Bondye do ou: fe pa ou, M a fe pa M.
God says do your part and I'll do mine.
　　　　—Haitian proverb

Contents

Foreword

On January 12, 2010, a devastating earthquake struck Haiti. The consequences of the thirty-five-second event included an estimated $7.8 billion in infrastructure damages and losses; more than 100,000 homes destroyed and more than 200,000 severely damaged; thirteen of Haiti's fifteen government ministries destroyed; 1,300 educational institutions destroyed; and an estimated 230,000 people killed, 800,000 injured, and 1.3 million left homeless. Never before has the western hemisphere experienced a disaster of such magnitude, and seldom has there been anything like it anywhere in the world.

This humanitarian disaster was unprecedented, and the response of the United States was immediate, massive, and effective. Within twenty-four hours, scores of U.S. military and civilian rescue workers and medical personnel had arrived in Haiti. Within a few days, hundreds more were carrying out rescue operations, providing medical care, and delivering food and water to the victims—all done in close coordination with our partners in the international community, the United Nations, nongovernmental organizations, and, of course, many Haitians. Within weeks thousands of U.S. citizens—military and civilian government workers, and volunteers from nongovernmental organizations, private insti-

tutions, churches, and humanitarian groups—had landed in
Haiti to help the hundreds of thousands of Haitians who were
injured, homeless, hungry, and thirsty.

The U.S. relief effort after the Haitian earthquake of 2010
will stand as one of the great humanitarian operations in the
history of the world, and one of the great achievements of
U.S. history. It is an example of how things should work in
a crisis. The mutual cooperation among the many groups of
aid workers was exceptional and highly effective. The fact
that there was no secondary crisis—no riots, no epidemics,
no breakdown of social and political order—is clear evidence
that the effort was a success. This success in the face of
unprecedented human tragedy owes much to the close and
effective collaboration of the many nations and international
volunteers who came to Haiti's aid in the dark days after the
earthquake, as well as to the determination of the government of Haiti itself. Above all, however, it was made possible
by the dignity, resilience, and positive spirit of the Haitian
people.

It is this resilience and positive spirit that Mark Curnutte
reveals in *A Promise in Haiti: A Reporter's Notes on Families and Daily Lives*, his excellent nonfiction work examin-
ing and documenting the daily lives of three families living
in the Trou Sable neighborhood of Gonaïves, Haiti. Modeled
on James Agee's Depression-era book *Let Us Now Praise
Famous Men* and drawing on his personal experiences during visits to Haiti between 1996 and 2010, Curnutte's book
humanizes a people Americans often view as faceless stereotypes—the Haitian poor. The individuals he depicts with such
care and thoroughness—a widowed mother, a teenager chas-
ing an elusive dream of a medical career despite his parents'
poverty and his own serious health problems, an unemployed
mason going overseas to look for work, a market woman

struggling to improve her lot, a mother mourning the deaths of her two children—are simple people working and struggling to live day to day in spite of great obstacles. Curnutte treats them with honor and respect and shows their innate dignity. They come alive for us in the narrative, astonish us with their resilience and optimism, their ability to make something—so much, in fact—out of such limited resources.

With words and photographs Curnutte shows us who the Haitian people are, how they live, and how they have historically encountered and overcome suffering brought on by poverty, natural disasters, and human violence. By means of this book we witness the faith, family focus, self-sacrifice, resilience, and optimism of the Haitian people. We come to realize our shared humanity with them, our common hopes and aspirations, our mutual joys and sorrows—despite our cultural, national, and economic differences.

I have spent much of my diplomatic career in Haiti and know the culture and the people well. Mark Curnutte's personal account of his experiences in Haiti provides an accurate portrait of Haitian life and culture, and I am pleased to recommend it to all who seek a deeper understanding of Haiti and its remarkable people.

Port-au-Prince   Kenneth H. Merten
July 30, 2010   U.S. Ambassador to Haiti

Acknowledgments

In addition to my deep gratitude and affection for the families who opened their lives to me, I thank the following people:

Jean-Robert Cadet, founder, Jean R. Cadet Restavek Organization

Doug Campbell, executive director, Hands Together

Reverend Dennis Caylor, pastor at my former parish, St. Veronica in Cincinnati, Ohio, and my first traveling companion to Haiti in 1996

Lucy Curnutte, my dear younger sister, whose influence on my life I still do not fully understand

Reverend Gérard Dormévil, pastor of Holy Family Church in Gonaïves and development director, Hands Together

Reverend Tom Hagan, founder, Hands Together

Michael Keating, photographer, *Cincinnati Enquirer*

Gary Landers, photographer, *Cincinnati Enquirer*, for his knowledge of Walker Evans's work and for his technical assistance in preparation of my photographs

Augustin Saintilus, interpreter, guide, and friend

Ross Spears, founder, James Agee Film Project, who introduced me to *Let Us Now Praise Famous Men* and the majestic work of James Agee

All my love to my family: Diana, Peter, Matthew, Emma, and Alexa.

Introduction

Dinner Hour

The bodies, some freshly dead, some bloated and literally baking from days in the tropical sun, had been removed from the streets by the time I landed in Port-au-Prince on February 23, 2010, six weeks after a high-magnitude earthquake shook loose the Haitian capital. Tens of thousands of unidentified bodies had been buried with heavy machinery in mass graves. Yet the smell of death remained—the unmistakable stench of decomposing flesh, of raw and rotting meat. The odor seeped from the shaded crevices of piles of untouched building rubble, overpowering even the heady everyday perfume of human and animal waste that mixes with burning charcoal and garbage fires to coat the sinuses.

The official death toll of 230,000 does not count the hundreds of thousands injured or the thousands more who would die from cholera late in the year, an outbreak feared by some but avoided during the notorious spring rainy season. The 1.3 million displaced in Port-au-Prince alone were susceptible to preventable diseases—not just cholera but typhoid and pneumonia, too—from sleeping on the ground in makeshift shelters fashioned from bed sheets and tree limbs, and from the lack of adequate sanitation and clean drinking water in squatter camps.

I spent ten days in and around Port-au-Prince, reporting

on the efforts of local relief groups there for the *Cincinnati Enquirer*. I traveled north to St. Marc, which had barely been touched physically by the earthquake, and five miles west of downtown Port-au-Prince to the quake's epicenter in the mountainside city of Carrefour. Residents there complained even into the first week of March that international aid groups had not arrived in the congested area, where shanties perched on steep grades and were accessible only by foot. I heard the same plea everywhere I went: "Mwen grangou" (I'm hungry).

The U.S. doctors and nurses I interviewed confirmed my layman's diagnosis: serious mental health problems, like many basic physical needs—food, shelter, and medical care—were not being widely addressed, despite the influx of several millions of dollars of global aid and tens of thousands of volunteers. Haitians were suffering from shock and post-traumatic stress disorder. People could not sleep. Some experienced stress-related seizures.

The depth of Haiti's need was at least recognized on paper. Fifty donor countries and major aid organizations pledged $9.9 billion at the United Nations on March 31, 2010, "for the next three years and beyond." But leaders of aid groups such as Oxfam say Haiti will reel from the earthquake for generations.

Haiti's threadbare infrastructure unraveled in just thirty-five seconds. When the earthquake hit at 4:53 in the afternoon of January 12, I was about to leave work in downtown Cincinnati. An hour later I drove at dusk through the city's College Hill neighborhood toward my house. Beside me sat my twelve-year-old daughter, Emma.

"What's for supper?" she asked.

"I was thinking about browning some ground beef for spaghetti," I said.

"Good" was the typically flat preteen response.

As I steered into the driveway, an e-mail buzzed my cell phone. I parked the car and popped the trunk latch. Emma pulled out her backpack. I checked my phone. An *Enquirer* colleague had sent me a note. It was an Associated Press alert:

STRONG EARTHQUAKE ROCKS HAITIAN CAPITAL
Hospital collapses in 7.3 magnitude quake

Mentally I went right to Port-au-Prince. The congested metropolitan area of three million people is in the same time zone as Cincinnati. It was the start of the dinner hour there, too. I could see the children walking home, dressed in their Catholic school uniforms, gingham jumpers or plain-colored, button-up shirts. They would mindlessly move around the tiny tables and stands of vendors, mainly women, who line the streets. If their mothers had given them money that day, they would buy rice or beans for supper. The covered pick-ups—called tap-taps—would speed past, a dozen people squeezed onto parallel benches in the back.

I had spent a total of six weeks in Haiti. The purpose of my last two visits, in 2006 and 2008, was to report from the northern city of Gonaïves on the daily lives of three Haitian families for this book. Gonaïves, which had 200,000 residents and was located about sixty miles to the north of Port-au-Prince, had experienced its own share of natural disasters. More than two thousand people died there in 2004 from hurricane-related flooding. Every building in the city sustained damage.

Good God, I thought, as Emma and I walked into the house. Now what? Was Gonaïves hit? With a quake that strong in a land where building materials are poor and construction practices substandard, I knew property damage would be extensive and the loss of life high. Hopefully, I thought, a lot of people were outside, not inside, where concrete roofs resting atop soft cinder-block walls would collapse to resemble a stack of dinner plates in a cupboard. As it turned out, the quake was felt throughout the Caribbean, but Gonaïves had been spared. A few buildings were slightly damaged—walls cracked—as far north as St. Marc, about a ninety-minute drive south of Gonaïves.

I made dinner for Emma and picked at a plate myself. Afterward, I sat at my laptop. I couldn't watch television. The first images from Port-au-Prince were too familiar: the upper floor of the elegant white stucco Presidential Palace collapsed. The Port-au-Prince Catholic cathedral, where I had attended Mass, leveled. The archbishop of Port-au-Prince, Monsignor Joseph Serge Miot, would be found dead in his office. The earthquake did not spare the powerful. If public buildings had been flattened, there was little chance for the tens of thousands of other structures, I thought.

The hours passed. The worst was revealed. Destruction and death were widespread.

With Emma asleep in her room, I went to mine. I knelt before a wood carving of Jesus carrying the cross that I had bought in downtown Port-au-Prince in 1996. Clutching my rosary, I wept hard. Dear God, I thought, how much more must these people endure? I prayed specifically for those I knew in Port-au-Prince. One was an American priest, the Reverend Tom Hagan, who founded the Catholic relief group Hands Together and lived at the organization's center in the Delmas section of the city. I had volunteered as a fund-raiser for Hands Together since 1999. Father Tom, age sixty-eight at the time of the earthquake, was a gentle and loving but tough-as-nails man whose fierce dedication to the most destitute had saved thousands of lives, particularly in Cité Soleil, the capital's most dangerous and impoverished neighborhood. I would learn the next afternoon that Father Tom was safe. So was Doug Campbell, the executive director of Hands Together. The Hands Together building, where I had slept many nights and eaten many meals of rice and beans, was destroyed.

The dozens of relief programs run by Hands Together in Port-au-Prince included a pre-seminary program for Oblate Catholic priests. Of the twenty-one Oblate trainees living at the Hands Together center, two died in the earthquake. Also dead nearby were the wife and three-year-old daughter of Hands Together chief of staff Nelson Jean Liptete, whose house collapsed. Nelson, who was thicker through the shoulders and chest than most Haitian men and looked like he could have played American football, had driven me once to Gonaïves. He had a quick, broad smile and laughed easily, though he didn't say much.

Hands Together also supported a series of eight schools in Cité Soleil. All eight of the school buildings sustained damage in the earthquake and had to be demolished. In one school community alone, five students, four teachers, and the principal died in the earthquake.

Then I thought about Augustin Saintilus, whom I came to know and like after I hired him as an interpreter during my research for this book. He spoke Creole, French, and English. He lived in a three-room, cinder-block house with his wife and five children on a steep hill near the mountains that ring the Port-au-Prince basin. Augustin and his family grew a small patch of corn to survive.

Our relationship was formal at the beginning of our nearly three weeks together in May 2006. A student of language, Augustin never failed to ask about the American slang that snuck into my vocabulary. He wrote down words and their definitions in the back of a pocket notebook. We walked everywhere in Gonaïves.

"I can't believe how people here get screwed at every turn," I said one evening after we had visited the homes of the three families.

"Screwed? Like a nail?" he asked.

I explained the lewder meaning of the term, and off we went into territory that knows no international or language boundaries.

"A beautiful woman, how do you say in American slang?" Augustin asked.

"She's hot, a babe," I said.

During the rest of our three weeks together, he taught me plenty of dirty words and off-color phrases in Creole, none of which I can mention here. We laughed like sophomores. Two years later, when I returned in 2008, Augustin would proudly use the slang I had taught him.

I was not able to reach him in the quake's aftermath. We had last talked on the phone before Christmas 2009 and traded New Year's wishes via e-mail, with him writing from an Internet café. I finally received a late-night call from him ten days after the earthquake. He had survived because his roof was made of wood, not concrete, he said. He and his family were living in the street in front of his damaged home.

Passion and dispassion—not happiness or sadness—define opposite poles of the emotional spectrum when in Haiti. You feel everything, or you are numb. You subconsciously shut down, blocking out the same sights and sounds that a moment before you hungrily absorbed. In the same manner, the scenery one passes while walking down the street can go from bawdy to beatific in a heartbeat. The tenor of conversations can flip in a heartbeat. One minute, Augustin and I noticed an attractive woman, and Augustin grinned in non-verbal communication. Then we turned a corner and encountered a woman sitting in front of a shack on a tattered plaid blanket. She asked me to take her malnourished child back to the United States. Another mother wanted to know my price to buy her sick baby.

One of the beatitudes common here is "Blessed are the merciful, for they shall obtain mercy." Acts of great mercy were evident throughout Haiti even in the best of times. One source of considerable compassion was the orphanage operated by Mother Teresa's order of nuns, the Missionaries of Charity, across the ravine from the Hands Together headquarters on Delmas 31. The children at the orphanage, some 180 abandoned babies and young children, were malnourished, and many had tuberculosis or HIV. About one in five died in the sisters' care. After the earthquake, a well-placed source initially told me that the orphanage had been totally destroyed but that the sisters, volunteers, and children escaped. Then I received more reliable information that the building had not been lost, though it had been heavily damaged in the back, forcing all who lived there to take refuge in tents on the street.

There were an estimated 380,000 orphans in Haiti before the earthquake, according to the U.N. Children's Fund.[1] That number increased after the quake, but no official estimate was available. The United States, for one, initially worked with Haiti's government to speed up three hundred adoptions already in process. Yet Haitian officials' fears of human trafficking were confirmed less than three weeks after the earthquake when police detained ten Americans trying to take thirty-three Haitian children across the border into the neighboring Dominican Republic. All ten Americans were eventually released, and kidnapping charges against them were dropped by a Haitian judge. The children, ages four to twelve, were reunited with their families, the government said. After this incident, the signature of prime minister Jean-Max Bellerive was needed before any child could leave Haiti.

In the immediate aftermath of the quake, the world watched Haiti eagerly—until the attention-span-challenged CNN mentality shifted its focus to other stories, including the stronger quake in Chile that nonetheless killed far fewer people, because of better building construction and adequate emergency response. Yet, like other Hands Together volunteers I communicated with after the earthquake, I wondered where the attention had been beforehand. It's not like a whole and healthy Haiti became broken and dysfunctional on January 12, 2010. My mind turned to a passage from the book *The Other Side of the River* by Alex Kotlowitz. It details the death of an African American youth whose body was found in the St. Joseph River, which divides white and touristy St. Joseph, Michigan, from its misidentified "sister" city, predominantly black and poor Benton Harbor. Kotlowitz, who would document the differing attitudes toward the death of Eric McGinnis, first went to Michigan in 1992, about a year after the body had been discovered and around the same time that Los Angeles exploded from the not-guilty verdict in the Rodney King case. The author wandered away from the spotlight to a more subtle but equally important tale in America's centuries-old struggle to reconcile black and white. Kotlowitz wrote that he didn't want to compete on the King story. I initially didn't want to compete on the Haitian earthquake story.

In addition to the suffering of the Haitian people, I selfishly didn't want Haiti to become the international story of the day.

Still, I agitated to get to Haiti, internally and in the *Enquirer* newsroom. My editor and I wrote a proposal for coverage of nongovernmental organizations based in Greater Cincinnati that were on the ground in Haiti. Feeling otherwise helpless, I prayed to be open to God's will. Less than six weeks later, I was in Port-au-Prince to report and write a dozen newspaper stories.

Beyond my humanitarian interest in Haiti and reporting for the book, I had traveled there in 2006 and again in 2008 almost as an antidote to the increasingly fervent Internet competition I faced as a newspaper beat reporter covering the NFL and the Cincinnati Bengals team. The topics were ever-more inane variations on a theme: rich men fighting with even richer men over gluttonous amounts of money in an enterprise that commanded a disproportionately high level of societal interest. I rotted intellectually.

In short, with this book, I wanted to learn if I could still capture whispers, not just shouts. Yet now Haiti is a loud cry. The rest of the world knows about it. There's a sincere drive to make its tomorrow better than its yesterday, sweeping sociological ideas referred to as "Haiti 2.0," which sounds unattainably neat and clean and a little too yuppie to my ear. One of the thoughts is to reduce the population of Port-au-Prince, about three million, to about half or two-thirds of that. Already, some 50,000 to 100,000 homeless people from Port-au-Prince have been sent to Gonaïves, stressing the already strained infrastructure and food and water supplies there. International aid, which in times of noncrisis funnels almost exclusively through Port-au-Prince, is simply not getting out to the rest of the country. The goal is to create new towns in the future that are agriculturally based.

Still, I wonder about the sluggish global economy's effect on the ability of well-meaning donors to follow through on their lofty U.N. pledges. There was also talk, not even three weeks after the earthquake, of compassion burnout. I experienced such a thing at the end of each of my visits there. I'd had my fill. I couldn't spend more than a few minutes at the Missionaries of Charity orphanage before coming home in 2006; I just wanted to sit by myself and stare into the distance. I could not digest any more suffering. When I left Gonaïves on June 29, 2008, I was sure I never would see it again; I had spent my last day there. But less than two years later, I couldn't wait to get back to see the people whose lives are detailed herein. Despite being a place filled with sadness and death, Haiti brims with life.

The families of Fritz Cénécharles, Johnny Henrisma, and Louisilia Louis have worked for years to make a way where there isn't an apparent one. They manage to feed and educate their children. They have deep faith in God, maybe even by default, uncluttered by the distractions of worldly wealth. I respect them. I like them. I hope I have done them justice by accurately documenting their lives.

I don't know what will happen in Haiti. I'm not an expert on food distribution, water, building codes, health care, sanitation, or any other item on the long list of challenges facing the hemisphere's most impoverished nation. Somehow, and somewhat negatively, I suspect that the status quo will re-emerge, and that 1 percent of the Haitian population, the French-speaking and lighter-skinned elite, will regain—if not expand and tighten—its death grip on half of the country's wealth. More than half of Haiti's people live on less than $1.25 a day.[2]

What I do know well are the minute details of the daily lives of three families in Gonaïves, families existing precariously—like the houses I saw on the ledges of Carrefour. These people are fragile yet strong, truly sustained by their belief in God, from morning to morning, season to season. The arm's-length distance reporters preserve to keep at bay the pain and tragedy of other people's lives has been breached. People with nothing on the world's scale—just a handful of beans and a cup of rice, maybe a few chunks of bread and a pitcher of clean water, a single banana to cut into six or seven pieces—have nonetheless shared all with me at their dinner hour. I'd known for a long time that Haiti was no longer just a passing professional interest. What I learned on January 12, 2010, was how personal it had become.

Chapter 1

Tender Lives

Beads of sweat rolled down my arms, the result of a combination of heat, humidity, and nervousness. Despite my efforts to wipe them away, one drop fell onto the black-and-white photograph of George Gudger. At least sixteen eyes, of varying ages, were on me and the book that I held toward my hosts. My paperback copy of *Let Us Now Praise Famous Men* was a novelty, not for its content, but for its mere presence here.

I sat in a plastic lawn chair in a yard that had not a single blade of grass, its cover the fine, arid, charcoal-colored soil of Haiti. Behind me stood, leaning and rusting, the tin shack that was the kitchen. Directly across from me, also in a green plastic chair, Louisilia Louis sat. A few months shy of her fortieth birthday, Louisilia was a widow with five children. The dominant features on her face were her broad nose and weary, dark brown eyes set far apart.

It was Monday, May 22, 2006. Four of her five children, the oldest four, ages seven to fifteen, crowded around the two of us. My translator, Augustin, my constant companion in Haiti, sat between us in a third chair. Oril Louis, Louisilia's younger brother, age thirty-six and a widower, paced around the circle. He held his two-year-old daughter, Micheline, against his chest, gently bobbing her up and down and patting her back with a wrinkle-creased laborer's hand. Oril's eyes, almost black, darker than his sister's, were fixed on my face. Even when I looked away from him, I sensed his intense gaze, clearly one of distrust.

I had come to Haiti in the hope of telling the stories of three impoverished families in one of the world's most forgotten places. My goal was to create a book informed by and paying tribute to *Let Us Now Praise Famous Men: Three Tenant Families*. The nonfiction masterpiece by James Agee and photographer Walker Evans told unflinchingly of the lives of three cotton farmers living in rural Alabama in 1936, renamed by Agee as Gudger, Woods, and Ricketts.

Now I was asking for permission to photograph and write about Louisilia and her family. The names would be real; I would use no pseudonyms. In addition to relying on Augustin to translate my words, I showed this family—the third I had contacted—Evans's black-and-white photographs in the front of the book. The first few pages came loose from the binding.

"I will treat you with dignity," I said as I slowly turned pages, trying to make sure everyone looking was ready to move on. "I want to show people who you are and how you live." I measured every word, talking slowly and awkwardly, formally in the first few meetings, so Augustin could follow me. Hour upon hour of this type of conversation would improve our rhythm.

Evans and Agee had traveled to Hale County, Alabama, at the height of the Depression to record the lives of sharecroppers for *Fortune Magazine*. The story, deemed "too unwieldy, too liberal" by the editors, was not printed in the magazine. In August 1941, five years after the trip to Alabama, the stories and photographs of the three families were published as a book.

I summarized the focus of *Famous Men* to Louisilia and

her family. Yet they were more interested in the photographs of the farmers and their children and wives: white Americans, impoverished, southerners, fair skinned, light eyed, living in houses of horizontal wood planks and creaking floors, sitting in the shade of porches away from the heat of the midday sun. Poor is poor.

The family of Dieudonné "Johnny" Henrisma was the first family that agreed to allow me into their lives. Johnny was an unemployed mason; his wife, Edele, did not work outside the home. They had five living children; two more had died and were buried in the Gonaïves cemetery. Two of the remaining five were living with a grandmother on a farm outside of Gonaïves.

The Reverend Gérard Dormévil, the Roman Catholic pastor of Holy Family Church in Trou Sable, had referred me to Johnny. Father Gérard is a development director in the Gonaïves area with Hands Together. As a mission appeal volunteer, I have spoken at Masses in Catholic parishes across the Midwest and South two or three times a year, asking for donations to assist the organization's human development work in Port-au-Prince and in conjunction with the Diocese of Gonaïves. Father Gérard also referred me to the second family that agreed to work with me, that of Fritz Cénécharles. Fritz was also an unemployed mason; his wife, Rosemène, was a vendor in the main Gonaïves market. They had five children. Fritz, a cousin of Louisilia's late husband, had then referred me to Louisilia.

I went to Haiti for the first time in 1996; I met Father Gérard then. By the time I returned in May 2006, I had been in daily newspaper work for twenty-two years. By January 2009, after nine seasons covering professional football, I had requested and received a transfer to the *Cincinnati*

Enquirer's local news section as a reporter. Newspapers have evolved—some critics would say devolved—greatly during my professional career, the start of which predated widespread use of fax machines. Now it's all about the Internet. The news cycle is no longer twenty-four hours; it is now measured in minutes and seconds. We give content away; we don't sell it. Yet more than the proliferation of Internet journalism, the biggest change, in my perspective, has been the institutional loss of concern for the disenfranchised. A long-ago motto of the newspaper industry, adapted from the Bible, was "Comfort the afflicted, afflict the comfortable." Now we comfort the comfortable. They, and not the afflicted, buy newspapers. They fit our advertisers' target demographic. We focus on the vinyl-sided ghettos of suburbia. The poor and often predominantly minority neighborhoods are only worth the occasional sensational crime and poverty stories.

Before taking my newspaper's NFL beat in July 2000, I had carved out a loosely defined urban affairs focus that included Greater Cincinnati's sometimes invisible Hispanic and Asian communities; undocumented workers; gays, lesbians, and bisexuals; and the poor, the working uninsured, and the unemployed. Since leaving football, I've reported and written in detail about female war veterans coming home from Iraq and Afghanistan, the spike in teenage homelessness, and the contentious issues surrounding the lives of undocumented Hispanic immigrants in the United States.

I was born in 1962 in Dixon, Illinois, Ronald Reagan's hometown. One of seven children, I was the son of a Nabisco cookie salesman and a stay-at-home mom, and I came of age in Reagan's America, a time when the president once wondered aloud whether the plight of a worker losing his job in "South Succotash" was indeed newsworthy. Against this national backdrop, Agee's *Famous Men* joined my personal catalog of go-to reading. It found company alongside Roger Kahn's *The Boys of Summer* (1972)—the story of Jackie Robinson and the Brooklyn Dodgers—as the most significant books on my shelf. I found whole paragraphs of Agee to be as beautiful and musical as any line from Emily Dickinson, Robert Frost, or William Wordsworth.

A Knoxville, Tennessee, native born in 1909, Agee was deeply affected by his father's early death and his mother's devout Anglo-Catholicism. They shaped his tragically short life and wide, voluminous body of influential writing. My own work almost exclusively has been in newspapers. My devotion to my late mother and adherence to the church as, at best, a cafeteria Catholic—picking which of the church's rules to follow and leaving others off my tray as I go through the line of life—bring almost as much pain as comfort. I recall with clarity the Sunday morning walks with Mom and assorted brothers and sisters to St. Patrick Church for ten-thirty Mass. Of the thousands of readings and sermons I heard growing up, two that stuck were the gospel that said blessed is the child that honors parents, and the one that said God cared most about what a person did with each given day and not what had happened the day before.

As a boy, I began to marvel at the voluntary manner in which a society held together, whether in my little town or one hundred miles to the east in Chicago. Today, I am more amazed that any structure exists at all in Haiti. Lives represented by yellow light glowing in the windows of passing houses also fascinated me—and still do. This interest came to bloom on a morning newspaper route at age twelve. One customer was an alcoholic woman who would berate me in her yard for being five minutes late with her paper, as if a schedule existed, but then hand me a bag of potato chips as a tip when I collected her payment the next afternoon. Another customer was a man who drove a maroon Mustang convertible. Over the course of a month, I witnessed a parade of women leaving his ranch house at sunrise.

Even in a town of eighteen thousand people, I saw the diversity of life, how difficult and largely impossible it was to lump people into groups. I thought about the existence of heaven and hell; I wondered how one gained entrance to the former and avoided the latter. Naive and innocent, I wondered, Why were some people rich and others poor? (I have never stopped asking myself why I was given so much.) Why wasn't everyone equal? I pondered my place in the world. I came up with a plan. I would work tirelessly and overachieve in order to attract positive attention, find self-worth, and overcome, or at least manage, my nagging insecurities over whether I mattered.

Beginning with my first reading of *Famous Men* at age thirty, I found some sense of place and order in Agee's writing. In an essay from the book titled "A Country Letter," Agee wrote about the individual and the individual's relationship to all people throughout time:

All that each person is, and experiences, and shall never experience, in body and mind, all these things are differing expressions of himself and of one root, and are identical; and not one of these things nor one of these persons is ever quite to be duplicated, nor replaced, nor has it ever quite had precedent: but each is a new and incommunicably tender life, wounded in every breath, and almost as hardly killed as easily wounded: sustaining for a while, without defense, the enormous assaults of the universe. (p. 56)

Perhaps we all bear the assaults of the universe, but certainly some bear them more directly and harshly than the rest of us. Armed with Agee's words, I searched out those kinds of people in my work for the *Enquirer*. Throughout most of my newspaper career, while writing about the impoverished or minorities or those who had otherwise been pre-judged or discriminated against, I could not comprehend the logic behind the attitude that the poor had chosen their condition—or that their condition was God's will. And the greater the distance between the comfortable and the afflicted, the easier it is to ignore others' suffering, and the easier it is to lean on the idea that some people are destined to suffer.

The late Catholic scholar Thomas Merton, a Trappist monk and author, addressed this issue in his book *Seeds of Contemplation* (1949). "It is easy enough to tell the poor to accept their poverty as God's will when you yourself have warm clothes and plenty of food and medical care and a roof over your head and no worry about the rent," Merton wrote. "But if you want them to believe you—try to share some of their poverty and see if you can accept it as God's will yourself" (p. 107).

Agee's writing inspired me, too, by taking readers so close to the lives of poor tenant farmers that they would be difficult to ignore. I first learned of the book from documentary film-maker Ross Spears, whose 1992 documentary *To Render a Life, "Let Us Now Praise Famous Men" and the Documentary Vision* premiered on the campus of his alma mater, Duke University. At the time, I worked as a reporter for the *News and Observer* in Raleigh, North Carolina. I covered the premiere and interviewed Spears in a park across the street from my office.

By late the next spring, I had moved to Cincinnati to take a news-reporting job with the *Enquirer*, where I had interned as a sportswriter in 1984. For the first six months of my time in Cincinnati in 1993 I was assigned to report and write on the simmering racial tension in the region, which would turn violent in 2001. During the preparation of a seven-day series titled "A Polite Silence," which would win a 1994 Unity Award from Lincoln University in Missouri, I read a number of books to further attempt to sensitize myself to my subject matter: John Howard Griffin's *Black Like Me*, James Baldwin's *The Fire Next Time*, Andrew Hacker's *Two Nations: Black and White, Separate, Hostile, Unequal*.

I also bought Agee and Evans's masterpiece at that time. I learned while reading that the book sold poorly until becoming popular with northern white college students and others involved in the civil rights movement. The second edition was published in 1960 to a more empathetic audience. Activists found a kindred literary spirit in Agee's social consciousness and unabashed idealism.

Some thirty years after the height of the modern civil rights movement—in January 1996—as member of a large, young suburban Cincinnati Catholic parish, St. Veronica, I was invited by my pastor, the Reverend Dennis Caylor, to travel to Haiti. Reverend Tom Hagan of Hands Together had given a mission appeal at our church for his work in Haiti. My pastor saw an opportunity for a long-term relationship. Students in the elementary school would study Haiti and collect educational supplies for children there. The parish would support the work of Hands Together with annual collections and donations. As a journalist, I went with my pastor to document what we saw and who we met.

When we returned, I prepared a slide-show program and began giving public presentations. Three years later, I was asked to participate in training with the Archdiocese of Cincinnati to become an appeal speaker on behalf of the missions in Haiti. I started in August 1999 with a presentation at a parish outside of Minneapolis. Since then I've spoken on behalf of the development group and Haitian church throughout Ohio, Michigan, Indiana, Kentucky, Pennsylvania, Louisiana, and Missouri. In researching and rewriting my appeals, I found some success with my audiences by humanizing the people of Haiti—focusing on the hospitality and good humor I experienced during my visit, not just the suffering.

Of course, there was suffering. For example, in 1996 I held a dying two-year-old boy in an orphanage for abandoned children run by Mother Teresa's Missionaries of Charity in Port-au-Prince. He was no larger or sturdier than my sons at two months old. I fed him a bottle. I burped him on a diaper across my shoulder, just as I did my baby boys. The Haitian child wanted to sleep in my arms. A nurse took him away. His bony fists clutched my shirt before he let loose. There were dozens of children that needed to be fed.

But there was also hospitality. During that first visit to Haiti I had gone to Pilate, a spread-out mountain village inland from Gonaïves in the north-central part of a country that is no larger than Maryland. It was there a widow named Maude fed me and two other Americans a Sunday dinner. She was the mother of a young man who had worked for the Catholic bishop in Gonaïves and had befriended the people of Hands Together. After driving for more than an hour, we walked another thirty minutes along a water pipe through some woods. Haitian children would emerge every few minutes to hold our hands or rub our arms, as if our white skin were a good luck charm.

Maude's home, four small rooms without electricity, stood on a small plateau. The kitchen, an open-flame grill that burned charcoal, was behind the house. In the front, a few bananas hung from trees. We were introduced. Then Maude, a tall, lean woman with an elderly face, handed her son a live chicken and large knife. With little refrigeration, game and fowl are kept alive until prepared. Five of us—Maude's two oldest children, me, and my pastor, and an aid worker— were asked to sit on chairs in front of the house. About an hour after we arrived, Maude served us chicken, rice, and bananas. The meal was sparse by American standards but represented almost a week's worth of food for her and her four younger children. Before leaving, we walked around the back of the house to say goodbye and to thank Maude again for dinner. Her small children were eating the chicken bones and scraps from our plates.

Those images, it seemed, resonated during my mission appeals with my listeners, who were perhaps predisposed to care because of their attendance at a religious service. Then the dots connected in my mind during the next few years. Frustrated at times with the relentless, around-the-clock competition of Internet sports journalism and other desperate measures of the newspaper industry to stay viable— and my own participation as a professional football writer in what broadcaster Bob Costas once described as "the toy department of human affairs"—I wondered whether I could make readers care about the people I had met in Haiti. Could I add the twin features of race and a foreign setting to Agee and Evans's challenge of stirring compassion in readers for the poor, white farm families in the U.S. South during the Depression?

I've had some modest success in my newspaper career. I am grateful for the many opportunities I've been given. I've worked hard. But the horizons were narrowing with age. I didn't want to turn from the golden boy in his early twenties to the graying man in his mid-forties who hadn't realized his potential. Life and work had to be more than an eighteen-inch newspaper story. I would borrow Agee's theme—that each human life is unique and, in its own way, divine—and apply it to what I had come to know in Haiti. I would not stay in Port-au-Prince. In 1996 I had visited Gonaïves. It had been the origin of several of the thirty-two coup d'états in the first two hundred years of Haitian independence, including the most recent one in February 2004. The 1985 uprising that eventually brought down the twenty-eight-year Duvalier family dictatorship also originated in Gonaïves. And it was there, on January 1, 1804, that General Jean-Jacques Dessalines declared Haiti's independence.

The city would continue to make international news. In September 2004, Hurricane Jeanne dumped heavy rain on Gonaïves. Water poured from the deforested mountainsides that ring the city. The sea rose. Of the estimated three thousand who died in flooding in Haiti, two thousand were in Gonaïves. Tens of thousands were left homeless. Every building in the city was damaged, and the Gonaïves Catholic cathedral was a refuge. The devastation was unlike anything relief workers had seen. Father Tom of Hands Together said, "I saw women carrying lifeless babies on their heads and staring blankly into space. Dead animals and people were floating in the streets. For quite some time, I could not even speak." Four years later, in 2008, and just two months after my second visit with the three families, Tropical Storm Fay and Hurricanes Gustav, Hanna, and Ike would again flood Gonaïves in August and September and cause the deaths of more than three hundred people.

I had found my destination. I had my idea. Like Agee, I would try to secure the cooperation and trust of three families. I would ask to write about them. I would photograph them. If I had just one book in me I wanted it to be about people and a place that I cared about. It would not be about football.

From his 1988 introduction to a new edition of *Famous Men*, John Hersey wrote that Agee wanted to reach the "unsentimental exactness" in his prose that Evans achieved in his photographs. Agee himself wrote that he had wanted the families to know he would "not do any meanness" to them (p. xvi). He told the families exactly what he was doing. I would do the same. I had an interpreter, but I was still attempting to communicate in another language and reach across a cultural divide. Could I make readers care? Could I make myself care? Could I see beyond my middle-class professional American life? Would I finally be able to use what I had seen, heard, and learned in Haiti to limit my complaints about challenges that I face, which are largely trivial in comparison? Could I see, ultimately, how much we had in common, despite our national, economic, and cultural differences?

More simply, I wanted to portray how poor Haitian families live. What are their homes like? What do they eat and how do they acquire their food and water? There wasn't indoor plumbing.

I had the backing of the local priest, Father Gérard. I had the endorsement of Hands Together, a group familiar to some people in the Trou Sable community. I took my paperback copy of Agee and Evans and explained how Agee's families had been poor sharecroppers. I showed the families Evans's photographs. They understood the visual better than I could explain.

In his introduction, Hersey described Evans's photographic approach to his subjects. He would let them "assemble and arrange themselves in any way they wished, and he would take his picture only when they were at ease and fully conscious of the camera eye staring straight at them" (p. xxviii). Yet Evans's work—both with Agee and his larger body for the federal government's Farm Security Administration (FSA) during the 1930s—has fallen under critical scrutiny, even more than three decades after his death in 1975. In short, the photographer has been accused of moving furniture or otherwise arranging or removing objects inside the sharecroppers' homes to simplify and beautify photographs. James Curtis, author of *Mind's Eye, Mind's Truth: FSA Photography Reconsidered* (1989), referred to Evans, somewhat derisively, as the "high apostle of documentary honesty" in a *New York Times* opinion blog in 2009. The seven-part series, "The Case of the Inappropriate Alarm Clock," an examination of the sensibilities of documentary art written by filmmaker Errol Morris, took its title from an allegedly doctored Evans photograph of the Gudger family mantle in *Famous Men*. Curtis's students at the University of Delaware compared Agee's arduously detailed descriptions of rooms and their contents to Evans's photographs.

Agee has not been spared criticism, either. In Part 3 of the series, Morris wrote that "Agee's prose was often an endless list of objects . . . at other times highly romanticized and often over-wrought." Evans's images, therefore, were viewed as more accessible. Agee wanted readers to taste, smell, hear, and feel poverty, grinding their noses into every unsightly and suffocating detail. Evans's photographs of sharecropper squalor were generally easier to digest—far prettier and even beautiful in their simplicity—than Agee's prose, many critics agreed.

Morris, Curtis, and some other scholars have questioned Evans's perceived personal engagement with the tenant farm families, too. Agree stayed in the homes overnight, and when he couldn't sleep, he wrote. Evans went to a nearby hotel. The journalists also had access alone to the tenant farmers' homes during the day, when the supposed furniture moving and other alterations occurred.

In Haiti, the three families always were with me when I photographed items in their homes. If I happened to shoot a candid photograph—six-year-old Dieuna Henrisma waking from a nap on the concrete floor in May 2006; two boys, holding hands, walking home with cooking oil in a small stainless steel bucket—I asked permission verbally or in gesture before raising the camera. The people always were aware of the lens looking at them.

The members of these families, I think, grew comfortable with me through the interview process, which required several hours over consecutive days, given the language barrier and the necessity of English-Creole translation. They had to get to know only one person, me—I was filling both the Agee and Evans roles. The familiarity that family members developed with me as an interviewer helped me gain visual access to them with the camera. As both writer and photographer, I sometimes captured images of items in the homes—for example, a set of shelves cluttered with dishes, boxes, and packages—for the sole purpose of having a visual record to help with detail recall as I wrote. Unfortunately, as an amateur photographer, my images sometimes were blurred or rendered otherwise unusable. The images in this book, like Evans's in *Famous Men*, did not initially have captions, but it seemed helpful to the reader to have more details about the people whose stories I was telling.

Often, I scheduled photograph appointments with the families. "How do you want us to dress? Where do you want us to stand or sit?" they'd ask. "Please wear whatever clothes you choose, hold anything you want, stand or sit where you choose," I answered. Using a simple digital camera, I would show my subjects their photograph. If they didn't like how they looked, I would delete it and take another. In one case, Nelson Henrisma, then age eleven, did not like how large his head looked in a standing portrait and asked that I shoot it again; I did.

I tried to treat the Haitian people and their possessions with equal respect. Evans had taken this approach in Alabama, as if objects, too, "had the right to defend themselves against the lens," Hersey wrote. As a result, Hersey suggests, Evans's photographs of the tenant farmers, families, and homes did not "propagandize squalor; they gave full scope to the timeless dignity, beauty and pain of rounded lives" (p. xxviii). I would find rounded lives, often in despair and a state of emergency, in Trou Sable. And the poor opened their homes and lives to me, just as they had during my newspaper work in four U.S. cities.

In Haiti, I saw the effects of a 67 percent unemployment rate and a 50 percent literacy rate. But rather than rely on raw numbers, I wanted to learn how statistics translated into daily life. I saw people borrowing money to feed their families and stave off hunger. I heard bright young people talk about the uselessness of their educations if they stayed in their homeland—not that there was a way out, mind you. The promise of Haiti's youth was unrealized and wasted.

I spent time in the markets, watching and listening. I was in homes, sometimes overnight. I walked the streets of the neighborhood several times a day, to the point that I learned my way to each of the three homes in a loop. Two of the families welcomed me as one of their own. The third let me in only after I said I would help them out financially, which I did; that issue is a point of internal conflict, even years later.

In the Haitians I came to know, I experienced neither victims nor passive helplessness. Buttressed by spirituality and faith in God, the members of these Haitian families exhibited agency—the ability to act decisively in the face of great suffering and daunting obstacles. The goal each day was to make something out of what an average American would see as nothing. The dignity of the Haitians struck me as twofold: enduring almost unimaginable hardships with little complaint, all the while planning and agitating to make a way where there appeared to be none.

The heads of the three households worked when and where they could, even leaving their country to search for a job. They controlled what was within their power to control. Houses and clothing—their only worldly possessions—were clean. The processes of caring for what was theirs were family events: sweeping, washing concrete floors, fetching water in plastic paint buckets, doing laundry by hand. Girls wearing shiny black dress shoes with delicate white ankle socks to school waited in line at the water well to rinse off charcoal-colored street mud. The Haitian people I came to know appeared to have taken to heart one of the culture's many proverbs:

Mye vo ou ni an sou pase ou rafen.
It is better to have a penny than to be broke.

Fritz and his family are my enduring faces of Haiti. As Agee experienced in 1936 in Alabama, I found one of the three families in Gonaïves to be the most open and engaged with the process of unfolding multiple layers of their lives. During my first visit, the Henrisma and Louis families were more cautious and formal in their dealings with me. When I went back in 2008 they were warmer, more comfortable, as if I had earned their trust by returning to see them. Sadly, though still holding together, the Cénécharles family had been fractured by Fritz's trip overseas to again look for work. The strain showed on the entire family, as the children had to take on even more responsibility in their father's absence, all the way down to the youngest, son Wisly, who was not nearly as playful as he had been just two years before.

Still, readers will find more details herein about Fritz and Rosemène and their children. Conversation, despite the language barrier, quickly became natural with them during my first visit to their house. We began to communicate nonverbally at times. We made eye contact. Simple gestures such as allowing all females to enter or leave a room before me were acknowledged, met with a smile or nod of the head. The younger Cénécharles children, curious about the texture of my hair, for example, grew increasingly comfortable with walking behind me and running their hands through it. Wisly, who once told me he wanted to go back to the United States with me, liked to sit on my lap.

Their kindness, hospitality, and sophistication impressed me during our first meeting, which took place on a hot, humid Saturday morning. Augustin and I knocked on the half-opened metal gate and peeked inside. Rosemène walked out of the freestanding sheet-metal kitchen near the house. We would find out later that she was preparing a dish for us to eat. Fritz walked from the porch, with Wisly, afraid but curious, following behind his father. We shook hands and were directed into a dining room that also contained a twin bed.

We talked with Fritz and Rosemène, as well as their oldest child, Mackenson. I was a novelty. My bare forearms, though tanned, were lighter skinned and covered with dark hair. I looked at my hosts closely through blue eyes.

At one point, Rosemène excused herself but returned a

minute later. She carried a plate on which sat a mound of rice dotted with small pieces of carrot and chicken. The custom was for us to eat it, Augustin told me quietly in English. He said the food was safe. We each took three spoonfuls from opposite sides of the plate. Even those few bites satisfied Rosemène's desire to entertain us in her home.

I was concerned that we would be given water from the well I saw in the front yard. I remembered what I had been told by another family: just because the water is clear does not mean it is clean. Throughout Haiti, waterborne parasitic diseases are the second leading killer, behind malnutrition. About 40 percent of the people have access to water that is safe to drink. Many wells are contaminated with human and animal feces. Throughout the countryside, people will bathe and wash clothes in the same crowded stream from which they draw drinking and cooking water. Providing safe drinking water is a primary goal for development groups in Haiti and other third-world nations. Hands Together, the Catholic mission group, bought its first of several well diggers in 1996 and has built dozens of wells for clean drinking water and agricultural projects throughout the Diocese of Gonaïves.

Now I noticed that although Fritz and Rosemène both took big drinks of well water from the same tin cup, they would not offer any to us. Instead, Rosemène gave a small blue-and-white plastic cooler and a few gourdes to Wisly. He returned a few minutes later with the cooler filled with a handful of ice chips and two plastic pouches of drinking water. It was imported from the Dominican Republic. Augustin told me the pouches would be safe and would not make me ill. We tore the corners off our pouches and drank.

Fritz explained to me on a later visit to his home that he knew his well water would not be good for me. He said when he was away in the Bahamas looking for work, he drank clean tap water. When he came back to Haiti, he drank from his well, and that water made him ill. Several weeks passed before his body adjusted to the bacteria. He said he did not want the same thing to happen to me, because I would be in Haiti for just a few weeks.

From the time of our first visit, Fritz and Rosemène clearly understood my project and what I needed from them. I still can feel his rough, calloused hand in mine, his fingers long like those of a professional basketball player. He often would squint his eyes against the sun and quietly pray without physical gesture. Rosemène was his rock, and the family's breadwinner through her small clothing booth. She was ever cheerful, fed by her faith and family, and fulfilled by embracing her day-to-day responsibilities. Her shy smile revealed two broken front teeth, one angled almost to forty-five degrees. She is an example of a *ti machann*, Creole for "little market woman" or "little merchant." Women are the backbone of the economy in Haiti and throughout much of the third world.

In 2006, Fritz, unable to find even irregular work in his homeland, was at home with the children. "My house is your house," he said during our first meeting. I told him that, given access, I would write about him, his family, and his community. He told me that it was God's will. Then he invited me to return any time.

Chapter 2

Gonaïves: Assaults
of the Universe

Assistance to the unfortunate honors when
it treats the poor with respect, not only as an
equal, but as a superior because he is suffering
what perhaps we are incapable of suffering.
　　　—Blessed Frédéric Ozanam, founder,
　　　Society of St. Vincent de Paul

Fragile lives already lived each day on the edge of crisis in
Gonaïves often rise to a higher state of emergency. The
cause can be a natural or environmental disaster or an
eruption of the political instability always simmering somewhere in Haiti. For a city largely forgotten and anonymous
on the world stage, Gonaïves and its 200,000 residents have
drawn international attention a handful of times in the past
generation.

Ash: "We Were Treated Worse Than Animals"

While Gonaïves might be difficult to find on a map, its location
at the bottom of the social order is clear. In 1988, the Haitian
government allowed four thousand tons of municipal incin-

erator ash from Philadelphia to be dumped from a barge onto beaches at Gonaïves. Under the guise that it was fertilizer, the waste sat near the water and salt flats for almost a decade. It was then moved to an open-air depot nearby. Pressure from environmental and human rights groups in the United States and Haiti eventually led to the ash's removal from Haiti. In August 2002, the *Philadelphia Inquirer* reported that month, the last 128 remaining shipments of the waste were finally dumped at a landfill in central Pennsylvania.[1]

The garbage's long, strange trip started in September 1986 when the Liberian cargo ship *Khian Sea* left Philadelphia with fourteen thousand tons of incinerator ash. Before 1984, the ash had gone to a landfill in New Jersey, but the state then decided to accept no more of Pennsylvania's trash. Initially, the *Khian Sea* intended to dump the entire load on a manufactured island in the Bahamas, but the Bahamian government turned it away. The crew searched the Atlantic Ocean for the next sixteen months for a resting place for its cargo. One nation after another—Dutch Antilles, Bermuda, Panama, Dominican Republic, and Guinea Bissau—said no. Finally, the crew convinced Haiti's government that the cargo was topsoil fertilizer, though the environmental watchdog organization Greenpeace would later assert that the ash was too poisonous to be used that way. In February 1988, the *Khian Sea* dropped four thousand tons of its shipment at Gonaïves. The Haitian commerce minister, when made aware of the true nature of the ash, ordered the ship to haul it away, but the ship already had slipped out to sea. The remaining ten thousand tons of ash ended up being dumped in the Atlantic and Indian oceans en route from Singapore to Sri Lanka, after those and other nations—the former Yugoslavia, Senegal, and Morocco—refused to take it in.

In the years that followed, various groups debated the

toxicity of the ash. Greenpeace asserted that it contained the toxic heavy metals lead and cadmium, which contaminated soil and air. Meanwhile, the U.S. Environmental Protection Agency analyzed the ash and determined that metal amounts were not high enough to be dangerous to people. Yet for the ten years that the ash blew free from the cinder-block bunker four kilometers inland where the dry ash was trucked as part of a cleanup effort, respiratory problems increased for some residents, according to Johnny Henrisma and others in the city. Diets were affected. People would not eat fish from the sea. Residents of Gonaïves said they knew the ash was not harmless, but opinions as to the degree of potential danger varied.

Johnny's eyes swelled shut when the ash blew in the wind. He became more sensitive to light, especially sunlight. Edele said she suffered headaches from the ash. The dumping of the ash, without regard for the health and safety of the residents of Gonaïves, was another insult not lost on them. "It meant we were not treated like humans," Johnny said. "We were treated worse than animals."

In January 1998, almost ten years to the date after the dumping, Greenpeace brokered a deal with New York City's Trade Waste Commission to return the ash from Gonaïves to Pennsylvania. A New Jersey company, Eastern Environmental Services—connected to the original firm charged with removing and disposing of Philadelphia's incinerator ash—had to provide landfill space and pay $100,000 toward the excavation and shipping of the ash back to the United States.

By April 2000, the ash was out of Haiti. But it would sit on barges off the coast of Florida for two more years before being returned to Pennsylvania for disposal. The U.S. Environmental Protection Agency and Department of Agriculture were among the many federal and state agencies that conducted final onsite examinations of the ash near Green-castle, Pennsylvania. Officials there were not worried about its safety. "We're of the opinion that if it got rained on for 12 years on a beach, anything still in it is not going to leach out," a local supervisor, B. J. Roberts Jr., told the *Washington Post*.[2]

In Gonaïves, there were no scientific studies to assure residents, just anecdotal observations. "When they took it away, the air was better here," Johnny said in 2008.

Massacre: "They Shot Two Men Who Had Crawled under Boats"

In 1996, on my first visit to Haiti, I saw a monument to the victims of a massacre that had occurred in April 1994. It sat on the salt flats at Raboteau, a neighborhood within easy walking distance of Trou Sable. The blue and white paint on the concrete monument was already faded and chipped. The memories, however, were still vivid throughout all the neighborhoods of Gonaïves.

Raboteau, a waterside slum laid out on a grid of dirt streets, like Trou Sable, a little farther inland, had been home to some of Jean-Bertrand Aristide's most ardent support-ers. More than two years after Aristide was ousted in a Sep-tember 1991 coup, photos of the former Catholic priest still adorned churches and homes. They would not be removed in the face of intimidation from the paramilitary forces opposed to the former president.

Then, on April 22, members of the military and the Ton-tons Macoute went door to door in Raboteau. The Tontons Macoute was the police force organized in the 1950s by for-mer Haitian dictator François "Papa Doc" Duvalier to protect him from opposition. It was named after the bogeyman in children's tales.

When the troops arrived, many people fled the neighborhood, but those who remained were dragged from their homes, the *Miami Herald* reported.[3] Men, women, and children were shot or beaten to death, then buried in shallow graves, where pigs and dogs later dug them up. Other people were dunked in the stagnant mix of waste and rainwater standing in open-air sewers.

On my visit to the monument, I talked with a sixty-three-year-old man who said he had survived the attacks. His name was Saint-Jean Louis. "The jeeps came in, and the soldiers jumped out with machine guns in their hands," Louis told me through an interpreter. "A whole barracks full of them circled the salt fields and started shooting. The fishermen [who had come in from a day working on the water] ran back to their boats. The sea is their sanctuary. The military jumped in boats and started following them. They shot two men who had crawled under overturned boats on the sand." Estimates placed the massacre death toll as high as twenty-seven people in Raboteau. The monuments inscription reads,

Peace to those who died 22 April 1994.
That their love for us will guide us to true victory;
    may their victory be realized.

Up to three thousand people were killed in politically motivated violence from 1991 through 1994 in Haiti, following Aristide's ouster—many of them his supporters.[4] During that time, a French priest, the Reverend Daniel Rousierre, living in Gonaïves, began investigating the murders. He and teams of international lawyers and forensic anthropologists exhumed bodies of the victims. The Haitian court had said to him that no evidence was available. During an interview in 1996, Rousierre showed me photographs of skulls pegged with bullet holes and corpses with lynching ropes still around the necks. Ribs had been broken during beatings with clubs.

Haitian Army general Raoul Cédras and high-ranking colonels ordered the executions of Aristide supporters, Rousierre said. Cédras, who rose to power in 1991, went into exile in Panama. Two other officers accused of planning the Raboteau massacre fled to Florida following Aristide's return to power, according to the *Miami Herald*.[5] Herbert Valmond settled in Tampa, where he was arrested in April 2002. Carl Dorélien went to Port St. Lucie, where on June 28, 1997, he won $3.2 million in the state lottery. Court records showed that he was to be paid in twenty annual installments of $159,000 in lottery winnings. Investigators in the Miami district office of the Immigration and Naturalization Service (INS) used lottery records to help track down Dorélien and arrested him at his home in June 2001.

By January 2003, Dorélien had exhausted all his legal maneuvers when a federal court in Atlanta lifted a restraining order that prevented the INS from deporting him to Haiti. He was jailed in Haiti but escaped in 2004 and has not been recaptured. In February 2007, Dorélien was found liable in U.S. federal court for "torture and extrajudicial killing" and ordered to pay $4.3 million in civil damages, in part from his lottery winnings, which had been held in escrow. In January and April 2008, $580,000 was awarded from Dorélien's winnings to two plaintiffs, including Marie Jeanne Jean, whose husband, Michel Pierre, was one of the Raboteau massacre victims. Jean chose to share her portion of the settlement— more than $400,000—with ninety other Raboteau survivors.[6]

The long struggle for justice was documented in the

award-winning film *Pote Mak Sonje* (2003) from director Harriet Hirshorn. The title is derived from a Haitian proverb: "The giver of the blow forgets, the bearer of the scar remembers."

Coup: Gunfire at Night, No Food in the Markets

The year of 2004 proved to be especially disruptive to the difficult daily lives led by people in and around Gonaïves. A coup that ousted Aristide—ending with his flight into exile in the Central African Republic—started in Gonaïves in February, and the region was hit hard by flooding associated with Hurricane Jeanne in September.

Anti-Aristide rebels—calling themselves the National Revolutionary Front for the Liberation of Haiti—first took control of Gonaïves on February 5 and moved south to St. Marc, where they burned the police station and looted it for weapons and vehicles, according to *Chicago Tribune* coverage.[7] Gonaïves was not their target, though; it was Port-au-Prince, the capital, where Aristide was refusing to give up power.

Still, Gonaïves again bore its brunt of suffering. As many as eleven police officers and seven civilians were killed in the first hours of the armed takeover. Food, already scarce and expensive, tripled in price. Roadblocks set up by gang leader Buteur Métayer between Port-au-Prince and Gonaïves jeopardized food shipments for as many as 300,000 people. Farmers would not leave their huts to go to the market to sell their crops. Besides going hungry, residents also heard the constant sound of gunfire in the early days of the coup. Families stayed indoors to keep their children safe. In the rural villages of Bassin, Magnan, and Brunette that ring

Gonaïves, work stalled on projects to irrigate arid fields and pump safe drinking water to peasants. Throughout the largely rural Diocese of Gonaïves in north-central Haiti—which was under the scattered control of antigovernment rebels—some Catholic schools closed for weeks at a time, preventing children from receiving what was often their only significant meal each day. In the diocese, which covers roughly one-sixth of the nation and attempts to serve many of the region's 1.3 million residents, Catholic and non-Catholic alike, funds were diverted from development projects to the most vital food and medicine distribution efforts.

Eventually Aristide resigned—a move he would later say was forced—and fled from Haiti. Supreme Court president Boniface Alexandre was sworn in as interim president. Enforced by an international team consisting of U.S., French, Canadian, Chilean, and Brazilian troops, an uneasy peace returned to Haiti following the coup. Yet the month's violence had claimed 130 deaths. René Préval was re-elected president in 2006. An Aristide protégé, Préval had been elected president in December 1995, when term limits had prohibited Aristide from running again. When Aristide finally was able to run again in 2000, major opposition parties boycotted his re-election, claiming fraud in the earlier legislative elections. Some of Aristide's former supporters now formed his most violent opposition. The buzz in Gonaïves among the poor was that those supporters had turned on Aristide because he failed to deliver on promises of power and prestige. Tensions finally boiled over, leading to the February 2004 coup.

Flood: "We Went without Food for One Week"

In September 2004, Johnny Henrisma and his family survived Hurricane Jeanne—barely. In June 2008, two months before Hurricanes Gustav, Hanna, and Ike would devastate his city once again, Johnny used a visual aid in the parlor to show how they had spent a harrowing eight-hour stretch overnight on September 18, 2004. He walked to the bedroom of his three-room house and carried out a crude ladder. The sidepieces of the ladder were not parallel, nor were the rungs. Made of hand-cut wood from a tree, the ladder had a skeletal look to it. But, Johnny explained, as he propped the ladder against the ledge that forms the ceiling above the side porch, where the roof began its rise to the peak, it had saved his life and those of his wife and three of his children.

His children had climbed up first, then his wife. They squeezed onto the ledge, bent forward at the waist, knees dangling over the top of the wall. "I stood here," Johnny said after climbing to the third rung. "We follow Jesus, so we slept in Jesus. We prayed. We prayed about the children and their lives."

Water poured into the city from the sky and the mountains that surround the city. The mountains are nearly white because of the lack of topsoil, trees, or other vegetation. Peasants cut everything down—and even dig up roots—to make charcoal to sell and to cook with. (Throughout all of Haiti, deforestation is a major ecological problem. Only 1.5 percent of Haiti remains forested, according to the U.S. Agency for International Development, compared to 60 percent in 1923.) The deforested mountains effectively create a bowl. As the rain fell, the runoff rolled unencumbered into the city. To the west of the city, the Gulf of Gonaïves rose. In some areas, the filthy brown water was ten feet deep. Sewers burst. Flood waters mixed with raw waste sitting in open-air sewage canals that snake through the slums at street level.

The water level reached five and a half feet in Johnny's house. It lapped higher than the window sill. From ten o'clock at night until six the next morning, Johnny stood perched on his ladder, the filthy brown floodwater splashing against his hip-high black rubber boots.

"It rained for three days," he said. "We knew the flood was coming because we heard on the [transistor] radio. Many people were sucked into whirlpools." The family had no food, drinkable water, charcoal to cook with, or gasoline. "We were just trying to live through the night," said Edele Henrisma, Johnny's wife.

That same night, Fritz Cénécharles was in the Bahamas. He had gone there on a visa in an attempt to find work to support his wife and five children back home. Then he heard that a hurricane had slammed into Gonaïves. He knew that meant flooding. Fritz's family, among the tens of thousands who would survive, climbed onto the roof of their house for safety. They took whatever clothes, mattresses, blankets, small pieces of furniture, and food and water they could hoist. Fritz's adult son Mackenson provided the muscle. The rain and wind battered them.

When the flood waters eventually receded, the suffering rose. "We went without food for one week," Johnny said. "People sent food here from other countries. But the people with food could not find us." In the adjacent neighborhood of Raboteau, U.N. workers tried to distribute some forty tons of corn, flour, and water but were hampered by unruly mobs driven to violence by near starvation. U.N. troops fired tear gas and rifle shots to try to control crowds.

Yet Johnny and his wife and children survived. Thousands did not. More than two thousand died in Gonaïves, three thousand throughout Haiti, from the floods and related mudslides. A quarter of a million people in the Gonaïves area were left homeless. Every building in the city was damaged. The bodies of the dead were stacked outside a makeshift morgue in the blazing hot sun. Finally, officials from the International Committee of the Red Cross had no choice but to bury the dead anonymously in a mass grave. In the makeshift hospitals, doctors stuffed cotton in their ears to mute the screams of the amputees losing limbs without anesthetic.

The stench was unbearable. In addition to the spilled sewage, the carcasses of pigs, goats, and chickens joined bloated human remains on the streets. Survivors plugged their nostrils with their fingers or pieces of lime or held rags over their noses to prevent vomiting, Johnny said. Additional factors also made life miserable. "We could not wear shoes; they would get stuck in the mud," Edele said. Mosquitoes were another problem. Researchers discovered cases of West Nile virus, new to Haiti and the Dominican Republic, on the island of Hispaniola following the 2004 flood, according to the U.S. Centers for Disease Control and Prevention.[8]

In less than four years floodwaters would come again to Gonaïves. I visited the city at the end of June 2008. Two months later, Hurricane Hanna would be among four major weather systems—including Fay, Gustav, and Ike—to dump heavy rain on Gonaïves in a thirty-day span, from mid-August into September. The chain of strong storms, resulting in widespread property damage and hundreds of deaths, was an eerie affirmation of environmentalists' dire predictions after Hurricane Jeanne that the city was susceptible to more natural disasters.

By the time floods from Hanna and its predecessor, Ike, had subsided, another 319 people in the Gonaïves area would be dead. The last blast of storm water would wash away the lone remaining bridge, at Mirebalais, cutting off starving and suffering Gonaïves from Port-au-Prince and international supplies from the south.

During my 2008 visit, I stayed at the Gonaïves headquarters of Hands Together. Ike and Hanna would unleash floodwaters that forced my host, Father Gérard, onto the roof of the two-story cinder-block building. The room where I had slept and the balcony on which I had sat and written in a notebook were swallowed up by floodwater. The only way out for Father Gérard was by boat.

Yet the immediate problem of the flooding, which caused death and disease, masked a longer-term issue: hunger. Following food riots and violence in April 2008, Haitian president René Préval had announced plans for both domestic and foreign investment in the fertile rice fields in the Artibonite region of the country, of which Gonaïves is the capital, the *Christian Science Monitor* reported.[9] The flooding in September of that year, however, destroyed the fields.

Chapter 3

Walking

The streets from Holy Family Parish to the homes of the three families formed a three-mile loop through the Gonaïves neighborhood of Trou Sable. The school at the parish was U-shaped. One end of the U connected to the church. The other arm of the U was shorter, linking to a cinder-block wall that led to an iron gate. A full-size basketball court was wedged against the base of the U and extended back toward the church. The free-throw and half-court lines were painted in yellow. Two wooden backboards with rims sat atop steel posts. The school had basketball teams for boys and girls. Practices and games were held outside.

The school building was three stories high. Exterior balconies on each floor provided access to classrooms on the second and third levels. Iron rails, painted white, ringed the balconies. Paint buckets, most of them white but a few gray, held palm plants on the edge of the balconies. Wooden classroom doors were stained dark brown. For each classroom, hollowed cinder blocks formed windows, providing cross ventilation. The roof was corrugated sheet metal, lined with rust-colored streaks.

Exterior walls were painted in alternating sections of pink and yellow between the floors. The outside of the church was a matching yellow. A line of coconut and palm trees stood inside the wall near the church. The bright colors and vegetation contrasted with the prevailing gray tone of the neighborhood.

In May 2006 I shared a guest room at the parish with Augustin for almost two weeks. Several times a day, most of the time with Augustin but sometimes alone, I made my way through the neighborhood. My route quickly became familiar, almost routine in the composite but made memorable by some specific events of Monday, May 22.

Walking out of the gate, I first turned to the left. I saw a piglet in a mud puddle near the school wall. The animal drank the water with its snout. In the same area of the street, within ten meters of the pig, a woman with her white blouse half open scooped water with a pail from a different puddle. She spread the water around the ground near the front of her house in an attempt to keep the dust down on a windy afternoon. A goat picked through a garbage pile for something to eat. I continued to walk and passed a white stucco preschool building. Representations of the *Sesame Street* characters Cookie Monster and Elmo adorned the wall.

The streets were not paved in the slum. They were made of hard, rutted native soil topped in dry weather by a fine charcoal dust. Piles of garbage, often burning or smoldering, were common. There was no garbage collection, and the constant fires contributed to the widespread occurrence of respiratory disease here and throughout all of Haiti. Pigs, hens, goats, and chickens roamed freely in the streets. (But try to take one that doesn't belong to you, and you will quickly be confronted by the owner.) Pigs grew fat on garbage and were slaughtered to feed the owner's family.

The street leading from the school ended at a woodworking shop, forcing a sharp, ninety-degree right turn. Inside the woodworking shop, which opened to a courtyard, three men used hand tools to build coffins. Six finished coffins, unstained, were stacked against a wall. The basic model of coffin sold for six thousand Haitian dollars, or about 850 U.S. dollars. A more elaborate model, with engraved, polished metal handles, went for ten thousand Haitian dollars. An unfinished dining-room table with four chairs and a china cabinet stood in the back of the shop. Small piles of sawdust rose on the concrete floor near the table, which was available for purchase. In the Trou Sable slum, clearly, coffins were in higher demand. A man asked me if I want to buy a coffin.

"Non, mesi," I said nervously in stiff Creole.

Through Augustin, I told him I admired his craftsmanship.

"You would die to have one, right?" he asked in Creole.

I laughed and explained he had touched on American slang. "To die for," I said, "means an American badly wants something. 'That house is to die for.' 'That car is to die for.' So, an American would say, 'I would die to have this coffin.'"

Leaving the woodshop, I took two sharp left turns. The road was uncomfortably narrow. Eight-foot-tall cinder-block walls rose on either side, no more than twelve feet apart. The sensation was that of being in a tunnel. Most of the traffic was pedestrian. Every now and then a pickup came through and forced walkers against the wall. A pool of stagnant storm water stretched across the entire width of the street. A pig urinated in the puddle. A young man on a motorcycle slowed and steered toward the water's edge to avoid splashing people walking nearby. A few utility wires crossed overhead. They converged atop a crude pole, nothing more than a crooked, fifteen-foot-high stick secured with wire to the wall and bending back toward a house. I turned right, stepping on stones as one would walking across a small stream.

Booths lined the street and were just large enough for three adults to stand in. One was called the B. and J. Lottery

Banc. These were not traditional banks or savings and loans. They housed a private lottery, a game of chance. A thin man sat in a wheelchair alone inside one booth. I acknowledged him with a nod of my head. Nearby was a square stucco building, painted blue, with the words "VIDEO SHOP" and "STUDIO PHOTO" painted in English above the door.

I walked to the right where the road met an open sewer line. It was a trough made of rocks and concrete. The walls rose about eighteen inches above street level and were about a foot thick. The trench descended another eighteen inches below the street and was some two feet wide. The smell was a blend of dust, burning charcoal piles used for cooking, garbage, and urine and feces—both human and animal. The stench became familiar.

A shoe repairman had a stand at this corner. Another young man wearing his hair in dreadlocks worked in a lottery booth. Beside him, a cassette player without a cover spun Bob Marley's "Redemption Song." It was powered by batteries. There was no electricity running through Trou Sable this afternoon.

"Bob Marley is very good," I said, nodding my head up and down. The man smiled at me. Marley's voice, despite the worn cassette tape, which had diminished the quality of the recording, was unmistakable. "Redemption Song" never sounded so pure, playing in this ravaged environment and among the people for whom it was written:

But my hand was made strong
    By the hand of the Almighty

There were many vacant lots in the slum. In one, a group of men who appeared to be between the ages of eighteen and twenty-two played soccer while also listening to Marley on a

Goats, chickens, and the occasional pig look for food on the streets in the
Trou Sable neighborhood of Gonaïves, May 2006.

Vendors sell rice in the congested main market behind the Gonaïves Catholic cathedral, May 2006.

More than a thousand students at Holy Family School sing the national anthem, "La Desalinyèn," during a morning ceremony on Flag Day, May 18, 2006.

Haitian parents grieve twice, a priest says—first when their child dies, and again when the child is buried anonymously in the Gonaïves cemetery, May 2006.

Unable to find regular work, Johnny Henrisma takes odd jobs, such as recoating a stucco wall he built years earlier, June 2008.

Tigar, the godson of Johnny and Edele Henrisma, shares a twin bed with another of the family's sons, May 2006.

With no indoor plumbing, the Henrisma family has its medicine cabinet outdoors, carved into an exterior wall, May 2006.

Dieuna Henrisma, six, wakes from a nap in her regular spot on the concrete floor in the parlor, May 2006.

Dieuna Henrisma chooses a prayerful pose in her family's parlor, June 2008.

Conversations in the Henrisma home are held in the parlor, around a small table that holds the family Bible, a stuffed rabbit, and artificial flowers, May 2006.

Nelson Henrisma and Tigar walk home from buying cooking oil for Edele, May 2006.

The Henrisma family on their side porch, including Johnny's sister,
Melianise, who stayed with them briefly, on her brother's left, May 2006.

Johnny and Edele Henrisma, May 2006.

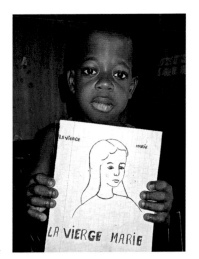

Nelson Henrisma, thirteen, likes to draw. He is shown here with his rendering of the Virgin Mary, June 2008.

Two of Dieuna Henrisma's friends, who asked to have their photo taken, June 2008.

Nelson Henrisma heads out to buy cooking oil with two five-gourde coins, worth a few cents, May 2006.

Tigar, Nelson, Dieuna, and Dieunel sit on the Henrisma family's side porch, the main living space in their three-room home, May 2006.

Nelson Henrisma, May 2006.

Dieunel Henrisma, sixteen, May 2006.

Edele Henrisma's kitchen is a freestanding shed fashioned from sheet metal, lumber, and tree limbs, May 2006.

well-worn cassette player. The song "One Love" boomed. The men, some without shirts, dripped sweat in the afternoon sun. The homemade goal, fashioned from scrap lumber, measured no more than two feet high and three feet wide. A few white clouds were all that interrupted the tropical blue sky.

My frequent walks through the neighborhood helped to immerse me further in the lives of the people who lived there, and in the larger culture. Looking back, I realize that I often dehumanized the Haitians in our initial encounters by elevating them to the level of one-dimensional deity, holy in their helpless victimization and poverty. But I grew more comfortable each time I went out—enriching, deepening, and complicating my relationships with them. Not that I agree, but a minor scholarly criticism of Agee's relationship with the poor farmers and their families in Alabama is that he too fervently avoided their shortcomings in *Let Us Now Praise Famous Men*.

People who lived on my walking route in Trou Sable began to recognize me. I recognized them too, adult and child alike. There were reciprocal smiles and nods. "Bonjou, Blan," they would greet me. (*Blan* is Creole for "white," a common word used by Haitians to describe Caucasians.) Children would want to shake my hand and wrap their tiny hands around one or two of my fingers.

Time and familiarity also brought me slowly closer to the members of the three families, reducing emotional distances and stereotypes and increasing mutual trust and knowledge of each other. We shook hands, we hugged. Young children sat on my lap, as my own children had. Women kissed my cheeks, putting their faces near mine in a formal greeting or farewell. I smelled the scent of their shampoo or a dab of faint perfume.

I tasted their food. I sat in their chairs and slept in their beds as a houseguest. We laughed and learned to gently joke and tease each other, even without the benefit of words. Yet there was one person, a Haitian woman in her twenties in Gonaïves, who broke down any remaining barriers for me, smashing them to pieces—like a thin glass vase falling to a concrete floor—so they could never be put back together. She was not a member of one of the three families. I won't use her real name or give her a pseudonym. She shall remain a pronoun. I saw her simply as a woman, not a Haitian woman. There was mutual attraction.

She spoke no English, other than to call me by my name. "Bonswa, Mark," she said. "Bonswa, madmwazel," I said.

We talked through Augustin. A high school graduate, she was studying to become a nurse and wanted to serve the neediest of her fellow Haitians. Intelligent and impassioned, she expressed a fierce love of country and wanted to contribute. She loved her father but did not approve of him having multiple wives. One Sunday afternoon we found ourselves alone, sitting on concrete benches in a humid courtyard covered with stones and filled with small palm trees. She wore her black hair, naturally wavy more than curly, short and most often pulled back straight from her forehead. Her white teeth contrasted dramatically with her mahogany skin when she smiled. Her teeth were irregularly spaced but generally straight, never having been corrected with orthodontia. Dental care is a luxury, exclusive to the wealthy, yet even the poorest Haitians have healthy, attractive teeth, clearly a benefit of a nonprocessed, low-sugar diet. Her smile revealed an underbite, which made her look both mischievous and innocent. She had a small scar and darkened discoloration on her chin, possibly a burn. The complexion of her skin lightened slightly on her high, rounded cheekbones, almost as if the layers of skin had thinned from being stretched, and a handful of barely distinguishable freckles dotted the bridge of her nose and the skin under her brown, almond-shaped eyes. Her pierced ears often went without earrings, though I did see her once in a pair of silver hoops.

I never placed a hand on her, nor intended to. The only physical contact we had was her goodbye kiss on each of my cheeks that afternoon, when she leaned her face toward mine, all the while maintaining as much distance as possible between our bodies.

I strongly considered not writing about her but decided to address the attraction because, in the end, what she and I shared cemented my thesis that all people are equal—despite the surface characteristics that divide us. We were merely man and woman, interested in each other. Neither language nor background could prevent it. I confided this story to a few other Americans—men and women alike—who had visited Haiti for extended periods of time. Almost all of them related similar experiences that had the same positive, gap-closing result.

When I walked the neighborhood after that Sunday afternoon, I felt less like "me" and saw the Haitian people less as "them." I wanted to let some Haitian people get closer to me and get to know them better. My personal investment had increased.

After stopping to watch the young men play soccer while listening to Marley's music, I walked two more blocks parallel to the sewer line. A woman carrying a bowl emerged from a cinder-block house that stood beside the open pit. She poured a putrid mix of human waste and garbage into the sewer.

I veered left, down and back up a small ravine. A second

alley—nothing more than a footpath—led to the three-room cinder-block home of Johnny and Edele Henrisma. Three of their five children, as well as Edele's seven-year-old godson, Tigar, and Johnny's twenty-six-year-old sister, Melianise, lived there. The address was Number 13A, Second Christian City. Johnny was not at home. He was out looking for work. My unannounced visit found Edele in the kitchen, preparing the family's meal. It would consist of rice and some greens.

The kitchen sat apart from the main house, just opposite the side porch. The kitchen's walls and roof were made of sheet metal nailed to a crude wooden frame. A few pots and pans and baskets were stored inside the hut, which had no floor or door.

Johnny and Edele's daughter Dieuna (pronounced "Gina"), who was six years old, worked alongside her mother, spooning rice into an empty metal soup can. She wore a blue jumper with Big Bird from *Sesame Street* on the front. Nelson, her eleven-year-old brother, washed the side porch with a rag and soapy water.

Leaving the Henrismas, I headed to the home of Fritz and Rosemène Cénécharles, which was about six blocks away. They lived with their five children at Number 9, Second Street Patience, in Trou Sable. To get from Johnny's house to Fritz's, I exited the alley and turned back to my left. The street was a straight shot, again running parallel with an open sewer line. A naked three-year-old boy walked past me. He had suffered a burn on the right side of his chest. The damaged area stood out, pink against his black skin. To get onto Fritz's street, where the sewer widened, I walked across a crude wooden footbridge. A pig attempted to find shade under the bridge in the cool slop. A group of about six boys poked the pig with a stick. The group's leader was Fritz and Rosemène's son Wisly. He had his mother's broad, quick, content smile. His eyes looked like those of his father. He was the happiest child I would meet in Haiti.

A group of six men sat at a card table on the street near Fritz's house. Walking closer, I saw they were sitting on splintered benches and playing dominos, likely for money. I approached Fritz's home, surrounded by a cinder-block wall with shards of broken glass extending from the top, protection from potential intruders. I entered through the heavy gate. Fritz was a stay-at-home dad. A mason like Johnny, Fritz already had flown twice to the Bahamas to try to find work. He was deported the second time. His wife worked as a vendor selling women's clothing and household items in the main Gonaïves market, about a thirty-minute walk from the house, behind the Catholic cathedral.

One of Fritz's brothers was at the house. They were trying to repair the family's used Honda motorcycle. It was white. A crack in the frame was sealed with gray duct tape. Wisly led his group of friends into the yard behind us. I was told that today, May 22, 2006, was his seventh birthday, but he didn't seem to know or to care. Most Haitian children, especially those living in squalor, do not celebrate their birthdays. Many don't even know their birth date. How are families to celebrate when there is no food for supper?

Wisly pretended to kickbox a neighbor boy. Then he carried his one-year-old cousin, Davidson, around the yard. Finally he handed the baby boy to one of his sisters and headed out to the street for a soccer game with his friends.

Next I headed to the home of Louisilia Louis. Leaving Fritz's house, I crossed the footbridge over the sewer at the end of his street and turned left. I passed more lottery booths, painted bright colors and standing out from the gray surroundings. Three pigs scavenged through garbage in a vacant lot. Nearby, a white Nissan pickup had been abandoned and was split into two parts, its cab and bed separated. It had no tires. I turned right on a main street, walking through one of the major market areas in the neighborhood, and back toward the school.

A man passed on the street without noticing me, a rarity. He whistled and smiled. He pushed a wheelbarrow in which rested a fifty-pound bag of rice. To my left, a woman squatted next to a blanket that she had spread out on the dirt. On it rested her baby son, no more than one year old. Half of the woman's teeth were gone. Her frail, bony frame was draped beneath a stained blue-and-white-checkered summer dress. She wore no shoes. Her son wore a yellowed cloth diaper and faded yellow T-shirt.

She spoke to me. "Blan, how much will you give me for my baby?"

I only could return a small smile and abbreviated wave. To do more would not show proper respect. A foreign visitor is warned by experienced American missionary or development group organizers not to show too much emotion—in other words, don't break down crying—in front of Haitians. To cry is to express pity, a negative reaction and sign of contempt that regards them as weak and inferior, placing you above them. An appropriate reaction is compassion, which is based in empathy—or equality—and moves you to want to take positive action on their behalf. Assimilate and immerse. Think deed over feeling.

Still, the sight of emaciated children—the orange tint of malnutrition in their hair, flies circling their watery eyes, ribs protruding so clearly they can be counted—is difficult to process internally without reacting outwardly. A child's cry may be barely audible at times, more the muffled expression of constant pain, muted into a moan.

I looked at this baby boy in the yellow T-shirt. I could

easily guess the short arc of days that he would have. I sensed tears beginning to form at the inside corners of my eyes. I fell back, physically as well as emotionally, on cold, black-and-white information as a coping mechanism. "Look up the infant mortality rate," I thought, writing a reminder in my notebook. "Make this child a statistic." I pulled down the dangerous veil that allowed me to record sensitive detail without the drag of sentimentality. "Give that data to the reader. You are a conduit. You can't change anything." I later researched a U.N. report. In Haiti, of every one thousand babies born alive, sixty-one die in the first year, compared to forty-seven worldwide and six in the United States.[1]

As I continued my walk, a teenage girl walked past me in the other direction. She wore a Catholic school uniform consisting of a plaid skirt and white blouse. She had a dark purple ribbon pinned to her shirt. Haitian Mother's Day was on Sunday, six days away. The pin signified that her mother was dead. I began to notice many people wearing dark pins or flowers.

Louisilia lived in half of a rented duplex on Second Jehove Street, which bends to the left off the main market street. She and her five children shared the home with her widowed sister and the sister's three children and one grandchild. Their brother, a widower, also lived there with his two-year-old daughter when he was not in the Dominican Republic looking for work. All thirteen people, three of them adult siblings, slept in two rooms.

A cinder-block wall surrounded Louisilia's house, which had a gray stucco finish, the same as the charcoal-colored dirt. Its roof was sheet metal. The metal gate opened onto a large dirt yard. The sheet-metal kitchen, the walls of which appeared to have been burned, stood in the middle of the yard. The ground was hard, packed dirt. A three-legged stool sat near the kitchen. In the far corner, extending from the house to the wall, a clothesline was draped with shirts and dresses. More clothes—underwear and shorts—rested on a bench under the line. A large bamboo basket leaned against a washboard.

Louisilia was busy cleaning corn cobs she hoped to sell in the market. The family had eaten the corn, and now she dipped the cobs into a bucket of water. I resisted asking the insulting question of what use someone possibly would have for empty cobs. Instead, I smiled and nodded.

After my visit with the family, I headed back to the school. The main street was more congested than any other segment of my walk. Vehicle traffic thickened—pickups and motor-cycles, the occasional sedan. Tables and booths lined both sides of the street. American soft drinks, Sprite and Coca-Cola, were available in sixteen-ounce bottles. Packages of Wrigley's chewing gum were arranged by the color of their wrappers in neat rows on a table: white Spearmint in the middle, flanked by green Doublemint and yellow Juicy Fruit. Women's blouses on hangers waved from a line in the breeze. A female vendor had arranged dozens of undersized limes on the ground and crouched over them, protecting them from passing foot traffic.

I climbed to the right, up a small hill, carefully walking around vendors and their wares, onto the street that led back to the school. Its alternating pink-and-yellow exterior wall rose above the rusting sheet-metal roofs of one-story houses.

Chapter 4

Mother's Day

Nelson Henrisma, eleven years old, intently finished his writing and spelling homework. He sat cross-legged on the side porch of his family's home, his notebook in his lap. His younger sister Dieuna, who was six, lay on her stomach beside him, resting the weight of her upper body on her elbows.

The porch had a poured concrete floor with a pinkish tint. Two unfinished, crude wooden doors were swung open, a cream-colored drapery with lace hem flung over the top of the larger one. The doorway led into the main parlor of the three-room house. Out of habit, and in deference to air movement, the family lived on its porch. The kitchen, a freestanding shed of rust-streaked sheet metal and wood, stood across a tight dirt walkway from the porch. Edele Henrisma boiled rice and fried a handful of green vegetables over an open charcoal fire. It was a good night. There would be dinner. The four children and three adults in the household would not go to bed hungry.

Nelson finished his lessons and put his workbooks into a worn backpack. He opened a notebook of graph paper. In cursive, he began to write a poem to his mother. It was Tuesday, May 23, 2006. Mother's Day would be Sunday. Then Nelson drew in blue pen beneath his neatly scribed sentences: a flower with four leaves on the stem, bending elegantly from right to left on the paper; a potted plant twisting upward with three leaves; a heart atop which sat two doves.

Dieuna asked her brother for a piece of paper. Nelson tore out a sheet for her. She copied his drawings of the potted plant and heart; in her picture, the doves kissed, their beaks touching. The little girl called to her mother. Edele walked three steps back to the porch from the kitchen. "For me?" said Edele, reaching down to stroke the back of the girl's head. "How beautiful."

Mother's Day is celebrated in Haiti on the last Sunday of May. Eighty percent of Haitians are Roman Catholic, a religion that honors motherhood in May in conjunction with its celebration of Mary, believed to be the earthly mother of Jesus. On and near Mother's Day, Haitians honor their mothers by wearing a red flower or pin if the mother are alive and white or purple if they are dead. Life expectancy estimates for Haiti vary widely, but the World Health Organization puts it at sixty-two years, compared to seventy-eight years in the United States.[1]

In Haiti, I came to know three women, all mothers—specifically, a woman who worked outside the home, a widow, and a mother who'd watched two of her children die as infants. Mother's Day brought into focus their lives and the life of my own mother, Elizabeth Curnutte, who would die from lung cancer five months after my 2006 visit to Haiti. My search for words to describe the strength of these women led me to a few lines from the poem "Women of My Country," by expatriate Haitian playwright and author Jean-Marie Willer Denis, better known by his pseudonym, Jan Mapou:

Blossoming with life . . .
In all the nooks and crannies of Haiti

Another explanation of the strength and diversity of many Haitian women can be found in *Third World Women and the Politics of Feminism*, edited by Chandra Talpade Mohanty, Ann Russo, and Lourdes Torres (1991). In the volume, essayist Cheryl Johnson-Odim cites a passage by African American writer Alice Walker to describe how some women in undeveloped nations have chosen not to use the term "feminist." Walker, in a passage from *In Search of Our Mothers' Gardens* (1983), substitutes the term "womanist" in reference to "a Black feminist or feminist of color" and writes that a "womanist" is "committed to survival and wholeness of entire people, male and female" (quoted by Johnson-Odim, p. 315). Third-world women, then, Johnson-Odim summarizes, connect their struggles as feminists to the struggles of their communities against racism and economic exploitation.

In Gonaïves, I saw three women fight in unspoken ways for themselves, their families, and their neighborhood against all threats. Despite the common battle, each woman was her own person. Our first conversations revealed great differences in personality, life experiences, and the embodiment of Walker's concept of womanist.

Rosemène's spirit soared. Her role as breadwinner contributed to her overall self-esteem and gave her a greater share of authority in her marriage. Edele, by contrast, struggled with her children's health problems, which kept her in the home for many years. The deaths of two of her children created about her a cloud of sadness, most likely untreated depression. Louisilia, widowed and unemployed, depended on a slice of her widowed brother's wages when he could find work in the Dominican Republic. Despite the loss of her husband and her prevailing sadness, however, Louisilia would be the most likely of the three mothers to have a beer and trade jokes at a bar. She remained determined to enjoy life, and her children and siblings, when describing her personality, pointed out her quick wit. Like many older African Americans I've interviewed in my newspaper work, people who endured Jim Crow and fought the battles of the modern civil rights movement in the U.S. South, Louisilia laughed frequently. Yet the laughter, I concluded, masked pain. In short, she laughed so she wouldn't cry.

Mothers are the glue of society—perhaps nowhere more so than in an impoverished country. The universal affection bonding mothers and their children knows no boundaries. Without the conveniences of developed nations, Haitian mothers spent a greater share of their time on basic life tasks such as laundry, food acquisition and preparation, and cleaning: Saturday morning, for example, was dedicated to washing clothes by hand in plastic tubs and hanging them on a line to dry, though people would also wash clothes throughout the week. Children in the three families I visited were given more responsibility in how the household operates than the typical American children I knew. They washed clothes. They swept the dirt yards with homemade brooms. If a teen child or young adult found even irregular employment, he or she continued to live at home and contributed financially to the family.

Throughout Haiti, though, thousands of children from poor families are sold into slavery as *restaveks*, a Creole term whose meaning, "staying with," is an attempt to disguise child labor and abuse. This practice did not exist in any of the three families, as far as I could determine. A restavek, most often a daughter, may be sent away because her birth family cannot afford to care for her. Other times she might go based on the promise of being able to attend school with her new family—unfortunately, this promise is usually false. Some-

times, the child will be sold for money. The Jean R. Cadet
Restavek Organization estimates there are 300,000 restavek
children in Haiti. According to the foundation, slave children
in Haiti are responsible for fetching water from wells, cleaning the house inside and out, emptying bedpans, and doing
laundry. Often restavek children sleep on the floor away
from the rest of the family and rise before dawn to complete
household work before the family awakes. The practice is
condemned by the United Nations as modern-day slavery, yet
it continues to be legal in Haiti.

As children, Haitians, like those anywhere else in the
world, dream of careers in medicine, the arts and en-
tertainment, politics, and athletics. They want to go to school.
Few children in Haiti, though, are able to reach those goals.
One reason is the lack of accessible education. About 40 percent of Haitian children never attend school, and only 25
percent of high-school-age children are enrolled, according to a 2006 statistical analysis of Haiti by the U.S. State
Department.[2]

Rosemène Adeis Cénécharles, born June 3, 1966, was
among the majority who did not get to attend high school.
"When I was a little girl, growing up, my dream was to be
an engineer, a civil engineer, to build things, houses, buildings," said the married mother of five children. "My family
did not send me to school. My father had eighteen children
with three wives."

She now supports her family as a vendor selling household items and clothing in the main Gonaïves market. On
the Friday before Mother's Day, Rosemène received a hand-
written poem from her youngest child, Wisly, who had just
turned seven. The poem was written on a handmade card—

a folded piece of construction paper—that he brought home
from school. Translated from Creole, it reads,

> Mother, you are the most beautiful woman
> Because you are my mother
> You are the most joyful woman
> Because you are my mother
> Mother, you are like a flower

Edele Henrisma wanted to be a seamstress when she was
a young girl. She went to general school for ten or eleven
years. These days, she said, she can only write her name, but
she can still read the Bible in Creole.

In some of my photographs, she chose to wear a pale blue
shirt with a matching inlaid pattern around the waist and on
each sleeve. She paired it with a pink skirt adorned with a
floral pattern of green and red. Other times, she posed for
pictures in a light blue, sleeveless button-up blouse with a
floral treatment around the waist. She wore that blouse over
a knee-length skirt with a geometric pattern atop a green
base.

She has owned her skirts and tops for many years; she
bought them in the market. She does not sew. Her parents
could not afford to send her to trade school to learn to sew
and make clothes.

"I was sad, very sad," Edele said. "When you love to do
something, you have a dream. I dreamed of working with different kinds of fabrics and colors. When I see those now in
the market I feel frustrated because I cannot do it."

Men and women fall in love. Across all cultures, one of
life's sweetest experiences is the excitement and
newness of finding a partner. Louisilia Louis's dream came

true on March 9, 1998, the day she married Jean-Claude Cénécharles, the cousin of Fritz Cénécharles. Jean-Claude was tall and lean, his widow said. He was in trade school and would go on to drive a tap-tap for the man who owned it. Tap-taps are vans or covered pickups, often with brightly painted wooden shells over the bed. The coverings bear a religious slogan, such as "Jesus loves you." Riders sit facing each other on parallel wooden benches affixed over the wheel wells. Dozens of people can squeeze into a tap-tap, so-called because riders will tap on the cab's back window when they want to get off. A ride costs just a few gourdes (worth about three cents each), much less than a U.S. dollar. Ask a tap-tap driver how many riders the pickup will hold and the answer is, without exception, "One more."

Now it was May 2006. I sat with Louisilia as she recalled her wedding day. Her daughter Ketia Brunel, fourteen, brushed through Louisilia's dark hair as she spoke. An American priest married her. "I was very happy on my wedding day," she said. "I had nice flowers. Many family members and friends were there. We had a lot of food. He wore a gray suit with a black tie and white shirt. That night, we made love. We were very happy together."

She remembers the cologne he wore. It was called Zo Zo, a French brand made in Paris. Louisilia hesitated before telling me the name of the scent. When she did, the Haitian adults and older children sitting in the room burst into laughter. Louisilia laughed, too, and blushed, her high, dark-skinned cheeks changing color, flushed with red. In Creole, one of the slang meanings of the word *zozo* is "big penis."

She and Jean-Claude had three children. Then Jean-Claude came down with Louisilia described using the Haitian catchall term "the fever." He lost a great amount of weight, then slipped into a coma and was unconscious for two months. Finally, Jean-Claude died on June 22, 2002. Was it tuberculosis or some other preventable disease? Louisilia did not know. I walked a fine line in interviews on how hard I could push for personal detail. Even though Augustin worked for me as my interpreter, he was first a Haitian. Not often, maybe five or ten times overall, I think my most uncomfortable questions would be conveniently lost in translation. For example, had Louisilia been married before Jean-Claude? If I asked, that question went dismissed and unanswered, dissolved in the air or absorbed by the noisy clamor of always-present children.

She did, however, remember his last words to her. "He told me I would have to try hard to take care of the children," Louisilia said. "I was not to count on his family for help." He did not have life insurance. "'You will have to fight hard,' he told me." Four years later, she shrugged her shoulders, tired, nonverbally affirming that she had indeed done what he wanted. Then she said, "I have honored his last wishes. His family has never come to see me."

During their marriage, Jean-Claude had given her numerous gifts: a gold ring on their wedding day, earrings and a chain necklace on anniversaries. "After his death," Louisilia continued, "I had to sell everything: the ring, the earrings, the necklace, the table. I had to sell everything to buy food and pay rent." She did keep one memento, however: his driver's license. It is the only picture she has of her late husband. Her other photographs were lost in the Hurricane Jeanne flooding of 2004.

Sometimes Louisilia's brother, Oril, is able to find work in the Dominican Republic, and he sends money back home. Once in a while, Louisilia will take some of the money and buy small items in the market behind the Gonaïves cathedral. Then she will try to resell those items on her street for a meager profit. Otherwise, she is not able to work outside of the home. She spends most of her days simply caring for the children and picking up.

"I have many people living in a small space," she said. "We must keep it clean." Constantly cleaning is how Louisilia maintains control where she can. Her house might get a few minutes of electricity each day. A single utility wire extends to a back corner of the building, which is made of a stucco finish over cinder blocks with a sheet-metal roof. The windows are open but covered in black iron grillwork.

She often goes to bed by eight o'clock at night. Without electricity, life is lived in the cycle of daylight. "I pray to God at night to give me direction," she said. "I have nothing to give my children in the morning. But by the afternoon, God sends me something. Sometimes I don't have anything. We will go one whole day without food." The Lord's Prayer, which she speaks in Creole and which then is translated for me into English, is simple and universal:

Our father in heaven, may your holy name be honored.
May your kingdom come,
May your will be done on earth as it is in heaven.
Give us today the food we need.
Forgive us the wrongs we have done.
Help us to forgive the wrongs others have done to us.
Protect us from hard testing and keep us safe from the
    evil one.
Amen.

Fritz and Rosemène Cénécharles have not suffered the loss of a spouse. The couple is still flirtatious, joking and teasing each other about their first kiss more than twenty years after it had happened.

I asked them whether they remembered it and could describe it. Who was the pursuer? Did he ask first? Where were you? Rosemène said she did not remember the event. But she recalled the time of day and the location when she committed her life to Fritz, who claims to have a much better memory. I recorded the following exchange on a tape player, which Augustin later translated for me:

> *Fritz:* We went to the same church. We met there. We started dating.
> *Rosemène:* We talked. We tried to date. We began to get close.
> *Fritz:* It became very serious in 1984.
> *Rosemène:* I did not have another boyfriend before I met him, but he had another girlfriend.
> *Fritz:* That is not true.
> *Rosemène:* It was about six in the afternoon. He was walking me home.
> *Fritz:* We were walking together. We were talking. I said something to her. She said something to me. I asked her if I could kiss her. She said she did not want to. I kissed her anyway. I went to her and kissed her. I was surprised she kissed me. She was a Christian. She went to church.
> *Rosemène:* Well, I remember saying to him that it was God's plan for the two of us to be man and wife. I accepted God's plan for my life. I committed to him at that time.
> *Fritz:* Her kiss was like paradise.

They were married on October 12, 1986.

We cannot help but to internalize our outward experiences. I realized after I visited Haiti in May 2006 and again in June 2008—and wrote what I had seen and heard—exactly how much my own mother had meant to me and what a force and influence she remains in my life.

I was drawn to the mothers of these three Haitian families. I saw in them the same kind of nurturing strength—the fierce protection of their children and unfailing support for husbands—I had come to know from my own mother.

Without premeditation or plan, I have referenced my mother in this book. It seems appropriate, then, to further describe my relationship with her. I have come to understand over time the void that her death created in me, how I had come to count on her advice and how deeply I enjoyed our phone conversations, whether about baseball (especially the White Sox), the news of the day, or my six brothers and sisters and their families. My world is a much lonelier place without my mother.

In my attempt to document in Haiti the similarities of people there and the United States—despite surface differences of culture, race, and economic standing—I could see characteristics of my relationship with Mom in the relationship of Rosemène and her youngest child, Wisly. His love for her was as clear to me as the dust from the Gonaïves streets and the unrelenting heat of the tropical sun. He wanted to protect her and make her happy.

My father, John Curnutte, who died in February 2003 after a stroke, is my hero. Yet my mother, I've come to understand, was a great source of stability whose greatest gift to me was one of the most difficult to give: consistency. She had rules; we followed them. She set clear boundaries. She was at home when we returned from school. Sometimes, she had baked bread. The meals were always hot. The clothes and the house were always clean. She made draperies that hung in some of the windows of businesses downtown. I saw her cry twice, once sitting at her sewing machine. The sight and sound of her weeping broke my heart and made me feel vulnerable to the world.

In July 2006, Mom fell at my sister's house in Dixon, Illinois, our hometown. She had lost her balance. She quickly became more disoriented physically and intellectually. The diagnosis was precise: brain tumors and lung cancer. Three months later, on October 26, 2006, she died in her home.

On October 6, I drove to Dixon from Cincinnati to say goodbye. I had a premonition on the way that this would be our last visit. I thought of her the whole way.

There's a rise on Interstate 39 in Illinois over a county road where the highway points north from Bloomington-Normal. From the top of the bridge, some of the world's flattest land spread out before me in a blaze of harvest colors, like an oversize autumnal quilt that seemed to stretch all the way to the next topographical recess, the Illinois River valley at LaSalle-Peru—Mom's hometown—fifty-four miles up the road.

Squares of brown, tan, green, and gold were stitched together by clumps of trees at their corners. A yellow sun illuminated a sparkling blue sky, interrupted only by some low white clouds in the farthest corners of the panorama.

As I steered north, the change of seasons became more pronounced. Leaves were dryer and even more colorful. By the time I turned off I-39 at Troy Grove (home of Wild Bill Hickok, the sign reads) some trees were afire with orange foliage. A combine moved smoothly along in just about every field I passed.

Winter always arrives earlier in my hometown of Dixon than it does back in Cincinnati, obviously, because of latitude. Things were no different this year, my mother's last. My sister-in-law Kathy met me in the front yard of Mom's house. Mom had just gone to sleep. Give her an hour, Kathy said. A few minutes later, as we walked toward the house, the nurse came to the door.

"Betty saw Mark pull up," she said. "She is very excited."

"Are you ready?" Kathy asked. "Your mom looks a lot different than the last time you saw her."

"I'm ready," I said as I pushed through the screen door.

As I rounded the corner into the living room, my eyes followed the frame of the frail body tucked beneath the blue blanket. It was pulled up to her neck.

Mom's big blue-gray eyes met me. They opened wide. She smiled.

"Mark, you made it," she said.

"Of course I did."

I kissed her forehead. She coughed and smiled again.

"How are your little ones?"

"Good, but they're not so little anymore. Emma made a card for you. She wanted me to give it you as soon as I got here."

"Grandma Betty. I love you. Get well soon. Love, Emma."

"Look, Mom," I said. "Can you see the little heart she drew?"

"It's beautiful," she said.

I sat in a folding chair beside the hospital bed. Mom closed her eyes and drifted off to sleep. I wouldn't get many words for the next few hours. She was in and out of sleep. We turned on the Mets-Dodgers playoff game on television. Treatment for her inoperable lung cancer had taken most of Mom's hair. She coughed a rumbling cough. She had trouble focusing her eyes because of damage to her optic nerve.

That night, after my sister and brother-in-law went across

town to their house, and Kathy stepped outside to make a phone call, I had a few quiet moments with Mom in the darkened living room. The nurse had just checked her vital signs and left the room.

I sat down on the folding chair. Mom opened her beautiful, big eyes and smiled.

"Mom, do you know how much I love you?"

She shook her head up and down to say yes.

"Do you know that I thank God every day that you are my mother?"

It was no time to withhold affection. I wanted to speak all of the words that might have gone unspoken for years.

She nodded her head again and said, "Yes. Mark, you and I have always appreciated each other."

Years later, I hold tightly to her words. They provide comfort and warmth, like one of Mom's knitted afghans on a winter's afternoon: we appreciated each other.

She closed her eyes, as if fatigued by the short conversation. Her legs moved gently, almost in rhythm, beneath the covers.

"Now I know where I get my fidgety feet from," I said.

She smiled and coughed through a chuckle. She brought her right hand out from beneath the blanket. I took her hand in mine and rubbed the back of it with my fingertips. I thought about the countless loads of laundry, years of ironing, meals prepared, diapers changed—the unrelenting challenges and demands of seven children.

I softly ran the fingers of my left hand through what remained of the brown hair on top of her head.

She smiled again.

"You used to do this to me when I was upset," I said.

She pulled her hand away. I put my forehead down on my forearm, which rested atop the rail of her bed. It had been a long, emotionally draining day. Mortality called. Spent, I closed my eyes. Just then, Mom started to rub the back of my neck and head with her brittle hand.

Three weeks later, my mother would be dead. As we celebrated her life—I wrote and delivered her eulogy during Mass—I took comfort in the larger order of things. I was not alone. Parents are supposed to die before their children, and the vast majority of them do. The passing of generations, bringing equal parts joy and sorrow, means children bury their mothers and fathers.

I stood at my mother's grave with my children, six siblings, and other family members and friends on a cold Halloween afternoon in 2006. My father's flat headstone, commemorating his service in the U.S. Marine Corps in World War II, was surrounded by artificial grass, its stiff blades a perpetual deep summer green, darker than the fading brown grass of a dry autumn in northern Illinois. The limbs of Bradford pears held stubbornly to their foliage. Oak and maple leaves danced in the wind atop the smooth, cropped lawn, freshly mowed and edged. I always would have a place to go to visit Mom and Dad, though my faith teaches that only dust remains of their bodies and the souls have spirited elsewhere.

Parents are not supposed to outlive their children, I thought, as I held my hands on my daughter's shoulders. Emma was nine with long blond hair. Someday—God's will be done—she would stand in a cemetery with her children and two brothers and their families, watching my remains lowered into the ground.

The priest gave the final blessing and sprinkled holy water on my mother's coffin. I thanked God for her life and asked the Lord to please spare me the unimaginable pain and heartache of burying one of my children.

"Take me first, please," was my unspoken prayer.

Edele Henrisma was not so fortunate. She endured the agony of losing two children. She is also the mother of five living children. Two of them live with her mother-in-law, a widow, in the country, and help her try to eke out a living on a small farm.

Edele's first pregnancy, she says, ended with a full-term miscarriage. The unnamed boy was stillborn. He would have been twenty-two in 2008. Edele then had three sons and a daughter, and she gave birth to a fourth son in 1998. They named him Denis. He lived for six months. He was a good-sized child and appeared to be healthy, though he was a quiet infant. His parents could not tell anything was wrong with the boy. His death came largely as a shock.

"After his death, my wife went to the cemetery," Johnny Henrisma said. "Someone said they saw her walking through the cemetery. But she does not remember that. She does not remember going to the cemetery."

Edele agreed with Johnny. She did not recall visiting the cemetery but said she thought of Denis "all the time."

Their next child, a daughter named Luna, would die at ten months of age in 2000. Her parents knew she was ill from the beginning. She was born with what her parents referred to as "the fever."

Luna, too, was a quiet infant. The doctors could not determine what was wrong with her, Edele said.

Their oldest child, son Dieunel, had also been seriously ill in 1995 at the age of five. He had fever and diarrhea. He suffered dramatic weight loss. He recovered.

"I had faith in God; we have faith in God," Edele said. "God helped us out. The good Lord saved our son's life. We prayed to the Lord for our son. When you follow Jesus, you have to have faith in Jesus."

Another son, Nelson, born in 1995, became seriously ill as an infant, too. The plates of his skull separated. The family took him to a hospital in Port-au-Prince. He survived. "Praise God," Edele said.

I asked Edele to describe the experience of burying two of her own children.

"The doctor told me I have a sickness," she said. "I do not remember what he said."

I resisted asking her about her living children's enlarged heads and stunted growth, two signs of hydrocephalus. It is a medical condition, affecting about two of every thousand live births, characterized by abnormal accumulation of fluid in the cavities of the brain. A common treatment, which involves surgical placement of a shunt, or drainage system, is rarely available in Haiti. A program based at the University of Miami's School of Medicine does provide this procedure for some children at Hôpital Bernard Mevs in Port-au-Prince.

Untreated, hydrocephalus is fatal. The cause can be congenital or environmental.

Surgery for Edele's children was not an option, so she and her husband made a decision.

"I will not have any more children," she said. "Me and my husband both are very sad. John always has a headache. It hurt us a lot to lose so many children. Sometimes I used to lose control. I would weep. I could not stop weeping. Now I do not weep. We have faith and believe that the children are now with God in a better place than this. We know that."

Like many parents in Trou Sable, Johnny and Edele Henrisma did not have nearly enough money to buy burial plots and headstones in the sprawling Gonaïves cemetery. A local priest said impoverished parents who outlive their children in Haiti grieve twice: once at the time of the death, and again when the mortician takes the body away for an anonymous burial.

In the cemetery, many of the concrete tombs of the wealthy are positioned vertically with the body standing, and some are painted bright colors—sky blue and trimmed in white is a favorite combination. Overgrown with weeds and strewn with trash, surrounded by a cinder-block wall, the cemetery is a maze of above-ground stucco boxes. The graves of the poor, by contrast, are buried horizontally. Narrow rectangular mounds of varying lengths in the arid soil, they are barely detectable, matted flat by body decomposition, with no protection from the elements and sometimes only a single bent twig or broken stick sticking from the dirt to signify the head.

On my visit to the graveyard, I came by chance upon two unmarked child's graves, squeezed between large headstones. Did they contain the bodies of Denis and Luna? Probably not—the graves were too fresh. Still, there was no way to be sure. The son and daughter of Johnny and Edele were buried similarly, like paupers in the potter's field, the location ultimately known only to God.

Edele had no place to go to visit them.

Chapter 5

Shelter

In the Trou Sable slum of Gonaïves, the second of the basic human needs—shelter—is truly reduced to its simplest definition: to protect. The shelters of the poor are constructed of inferior homemade cinder blocks. They are susceptible to corrosion from saltwater floods that arrive with increasing regularity. A poured concrete slab that elevates inhabitants a foot or more off ground is a luxury. Dirt floors are not uncommon.

Exterior walls made of cinder block or rusting corrugated sheet metal surround the property. Rather than bug-proof screens, metal bars or specially formed vented cinder-block pieces, a distant relative of lattice work, cover most windows. These homes do not have indoor plumbing or flush toilets. Discarded outdoor furniture made of heavy plastic holds up well and is popular inside the open-air Haitian homes. Everything from furniture to clothing to cooking utensils and plates is purchased used.

Yet to see only the limited scale or simplicity of materials and design would be to miss the great effort involved in the building or acquisition of a house. To try to assign a foreign monetary value to one of those houses based on market price would be to ignore the thought that goes into the selection and arrangement of its contents. There is order and cleanliness where an outsider might expect to find only chaos and filth.

By U.S. standards—and even among her fellow Haitians— Edele Henrisma has few worldly possessions. She lives in a three-room cinder-block house with her husband, Johnny, and three of their children. She treats each piece of furniture and clothing, dish, cooking utensil, and wall hanging with care. Nothing is positioned accidentally in her home. Each item is important to her.

Edele's kitchen is a freestanding shack with sheet-metal walls. A charcoal pile below a stainless steel grill serves as the stove. One of the kitchen walls is covered with a complete sheet of metal. Elsewhere the metal sheets are a patchwork of sizes and shapes, running both horizontally and vertically. Edele does not have a refrigerator. The house receives about fifteen minutes of electricity each afternoon through a threadbare overhead wire. The kitchen has no floor, so when it rains, which it does often in Gonaïves, Edele stands on slick mud. Her kitchen is inside the protective wall that encircles the small plot of land on which her home stands. The outside wall is fashioned from the same corrugated sheet metal as the kitchen and framed with the same faded, dried, splintering wood. Though they have little, the Henrisma family fears robbery. A rusting segment of black iron chain secures the front gate. A link is placed on a nail in such a way that it cannot be opened from the outside. One of the adults or the oldest son will secure it each night. The wall keeps out animals, too, the goats, chickens, and pigs belonging to their neighbors that wander free.

The center of family life is the side porch. It is across a dirt patch from the kitchen. The porch is one step up from the ground and leads into the parlor. Johnny scratches together a living through odd jobs and perpetual borrowing; he built his family's house. The double doors leading into the house from the side porch are not the same size, though close to it, showing his intent to make them symmetrical. On the inside, Edele had hung a cream-colored lace curtain. She bunched and pulled it back outside, positioning it over the top of one of the wooden doors to allow air to flow through. When he built the house, Johnny punched a horizontal window in the wall opposite the doors and of the same width. A red lace curtain hangs from a rod. Special cinder-block windows allow air to come in. They were made by pouring cement mix into a mold that forms spokelike spindles extending from the center.

On either side of the doors on the porch, Johnny carved a shelf out of the cinder-block wall. The shelves are arched at the top and measure about eighteen inches across the bottom. They serve almost as outdoor medicine cabinets. In one rests nail clippers and a bottle that once held liquid medicine and lists an expiration date of 2005.

Inside, between the doors and the parlor window, Edele placed the centerpiece of her room—a low, green, plastic yard table. It is square. She covered it with a white lace cloth and arranged on it the family Bible, a Catholic hymnal, a white vase from which rise plastic and paper roses colored red, yellow, and white, and a stuffed rabbit. The rabbit is the family pet. In Creole, the word for this kind of this nonliving pet is *nou nous*. (Louisilia Louis and her family have their own nou nous—a stuffed Kermit the Frog.)

Haitian women are fond of flowers, though the only kind found in the slums are artificial. They symbolically take on greater meaning given the environment. Against a backdrop that is largely gray—cinder-block houses and walls, rusted sheet metal, and charcoal-colored streets that turn black in rain—the flowers bring color, light, and life into spaces that are otherwise visually bland. Women might not be able to change the larger environment, but the smaller spaces inside their homes are another matter. When Edele posed for a photograph with her husband, she wanted to hold some of the colorful fake flowers.

A rosary of alternating red and yellow beads—leading to a white crucifix—hangs from the thick green stem of one of Edele's artificial parlor roses. Around the center table, Edele arranged four matching green lawn chairs. We sat there to talk. I was given the seat nearest the window and farthest from the doors, with Johnny directly across from me, Edele to my left, and Augustin to my right. I put my cassette recorder on top of the Bible.

To my right, three white chairs with mesh metal backs and wooden seats were lined up against the back wall. They were part of the set that had been replaced by the green furniture. Children would sit on the white chairs if they wanted to listen to our conversations. In that corner, Edele had hung three stainless steel cooking pots. She hooked each handle over a large nail that had been driven into the finished stucco wall.

To my left was a white wire rack with three shelves. On it, Edele arranged her dishes. Two identical serving trays, painted white and framed with apples, leaned against the wall. In front of them, Edele stacked plastic cups and metal plates and bowls. On the bottom shelf she stored an electric cooking pot, a coffeemaker, a tea kettle, and three plastic water pitchers. She draped flowered sheets from each shelf that she could roll down in an attempt to keep her dishes clean in the open-air house. In this and many other homes in the Trou Sable slum, dishes are washed before and after meals. The air is filled with dust and smoke.

Continuing around the room, on the front wall to the left of my chair, a battery-powered clock hangs from a nail. The clock's face shows a scene, against a backdrop of serene blue, of the Last Supper of Jesus. Jesus, like his disciples, is painted as a white man. The clock's hands are frozen in time, at 10:46. Centered beneath the clock is a white lawn table that matches the three extra chairs across the room. On the table sits the family's second nou nous, a tan stuffed cat.

Doors lead to bedrooms on each side of the parlor, at the front and back of the house. In the front room, two twin beds are wedged into corners, white sheets covering them. The metal bed frames are elevated on rocks. The floor is finished concrete but not with the same light red colored swirls mixed in as the parlor. A white curtain with hearts of pink and red stitching hangs in front of a window. A series of hooks extend from a block of wood affixed to the cinder-block wall. From the hooks the children hang their backpacks and a few pieces of clothing. A nineteen-inch black-and-white television set, unplugged, sits atop a crude small wooden table between the beds.

Johnny and Edele sleep in a queen-size bed in the back bedroom. A sheet can be pulled along a wire to shield the bed from the rest of the room. There is a kitchen table against the back wall of the house. The walls in the bedrooms are partially finished with a coating that is gray and unpainted. Where they are not covered, the walls are exposed gray cinder block and darker gray mortar. The floor in the back bedroom is unfinished. It is made of rocks that have not been filled with concrete. A radio rests on the table. It has a twin cassette deck. The antenna is missing, replaced by a rusting white metal clothes hanger and a wire running up to an exposed ceiling truss. The radio is tuned to a station that plays religious music. When electricity does pulse into the house, the immediate blaring sound of music—punctuated by static from the poor reception—is startling to visitors. The family is accustomed to it, though, and appears to take comfort in its regularity.

Johnny stores some tools in his bedroom. He has a white hard hat. There is a level, a square, two measuring tapes, a hammer, and two saw blades: one for wood, another for metal. He built the house, starting with the fence. Johnny tried leaves from coconut trees, but they would not keep out animals. He bought corrugated metal sheets and wood. The project took him three days to complete. Once the lot was fenced in, he went about constructing the foundation, which would be called a slab in the United States. He laid out the foundation edge in cinder block, securing it with mortar. From each corner, Johnny planted rebar rods in the wet concrete; he would later pour cement posts around the iron. In between the posts he would build cinder-block walls. Wherever an internal or external wall would rise, Johnny supported it with a cinder-block base. Where he would eventually pour concrete floors, he placed rocks and stone as fill.

He bought his materials—rock, sand, and cement mix—on credit. The water he hauled from a nearby well. The walls took a year to construct. The roof—peaked and running from the front to the back of the house—is supported by homemade wooden trusses that are not the finished, squared lumber secured with metal brackets familiar in the United States. The trusses of this Haitian house are thick sticks that pass as lumber. They are crooked. The roof is not flush to the top of the walls. There is a gap through which air flows and light enters during the day.

Johnny said he and his family moved into the house December 2, 2000. They had been living in a rented house nearby. Edele said that two weeks and a day after they moved in, their daughter, Luna, only ten months at the time, died.

There is no running water. The family members walk

about a quarter of a mile to a well to fill old paint buckets. They pour unheated water over themselves to bathe. People are impeccably clean in Haiti, though; they shower frequently. Water is otherwise heated in stainless steel pots over a charcoal fire for cooking.

Behind Johnny's house, inside the wall, he dug out a four-by-four-foot open-air latrine that rises about three feet above the ground. It is constructed of the same cinder block used to build the house. Males can stand to urinate into the pit. People sit on the top of the wall to defecate. There is no toilet paper, unless an impoverished Haitian is trying to impress a guest. People use scraps of paper, newspaper, or old rags torn into strips to clean themselves.

Bayakou is a Creole word for a latrine cleaner. These people work at night when the family is asleep. Arrangements are made in advance. The bayakou goes down into the latrine and hauls out the feces, any standing water, and waste paper in buckets.

There are no master bathrooms or kids' bathrooms in the home of a poor Haitian family. In fact, children in Haiti rarely have their own bedrooms. Many children in the Trou Sable slum don't have their own bed.

Louisilia Louis, her widowed sister, widowed brother, and their combined nine children and one grandchild live in a two-room rented house. The metal bedposts are propped up on pieces of cinder block, creating more space under the bed. In times of relentless heat and humidity, which are often, the extra space allows people to sleep on the cooler concrete floor.

In the main room, where two twin beds are divided by the main entrance to the home and form a makeshift hallway, Louisilia's sister, Dieumène, has her sleeping spot on the floor between the beds. Her three children and one grandchild

share the two beds on either side of her. Two children sleep
on a mat at her head. A small hallway and a closet lead to
the house's only other room. Louisilia and Oril, her brother,
share a queen-size bed. Four children sleep in assigned spots
on the concrete floor. Oril often is in the Dominican Republic,
where he is better able to find work.

Compared to the homes of his friend Johnny Henrisma and Louisilia Louis, the widow of his cousin, Fritz
Cénécharles and his family live in an elaborate one. Fritz's
two-wing home is painted tan and with two peaked stripes
of red that run parallel with the pitch of the roof. The house
is surrounded by a cinder-block wall topped with shards of
broken glass; a rust-colored iron gate in the front is locked
at night, yet neighbors enter at all times of the day with paint
buckets they fill with water from his well. He does not charge
them. Most people who own a well will make even their next-
door neighbors give them a few cents for a paint bucket of
water.

The house took Fritz eight years to complete. He told me
with pride that he built every inch of the home. He is a skilled
mason who nonetheless cannot find steady work, just odd
jobs. His wife, Rosemène, sells household goods and clothing
in the market. She has access to credit through her business,
so as a result, her family has a larger house and more possessions—more clothing, furniture, and household items.

The main living area of the house is positioned in the back
southwest corner of the lot, which measures roughly forty
feet wide by fifty-three feet deep. It consists of three rooms—
a dining room with a used wooden dining table and four
chairs, a china cabinet, and a twin bed shared by the two
youngest children, Rosena and Wisly. The family's nou nous
reclines on the bed. It is a cream-and-black-striped tiger.

The furniture has an oak finish. The wood feels soft and

damp, almost swollen to the touch, the result of Caribbean humidity. Rosemène placed an arrangement of red and white plastic flowers in a vase at the center of the table. The cabinet is filled with assorted dishes, cups, glasses, plastic cups, plastic pitchers, and serving bowls. A string of rosary beads hangs from a nail front and center. A small bottle of vitamins for Fritz sits on the bottom shelf.

The dining room runs the length of the building, about seventeen feet. Off to the left is the master bedroom. It is dominated by a queen-size bed, covered in a white sheet, and his-and-her dressers. In the corner is a suitcase with a luggage tag from Port-au-Prince to Nassau, Bahamas. Fritz had gone there looking for work. To the front of the bedroom, through a door, is the parlor. It is crowded with a couch, two chairs, and a large set of shelves, upon which rests a television set that goes unused because of the lack of electricity. The whole house has finished concrete floors. The living wing has an artificial hung ceiling of alternating cream and light red tiles, stained by rainwater. The stucco walls are painted tan. The parlor has a screened front window, covered on the outside by iron bars. A door leads out of the front of the parlor to a covered porch.

Along the north side of the property Fritz built a wing with two bedrooms. The roof pitch runs water toward the center of the property, away from the outside wall. The oldest son, Mackenson, shares the larger of the two rooms with the oldest daughter, Nadège. A table covered with a green gingham plastic tablecloth divides the two twin beds. Clothes are folded and stacked in thin brown garbage bags on corner tables. Another daughter, Fritzlande, sleeps in a twin bed in the smaller room, which measures about eight feet by seven feet. A large blackboard, framed in wood, is screwed into the west wall.

Like the main wing, the sleeping wing is elevated on a slab of finished concrete and has a porch running in front of the two bedrooms. An enclosed shower is attached to the bedrooms, and in the corner is a two-seat latrine, also covered and walled. There is open space between the two, and Fritz said he planned to build a permanent kitchen, removing the shed from the front yard—when he could scrape the money together.

Chapter 6

Money

The average Haitian lives on less than two U.S. dollars a day. Those couple of dollars encompass the cost of all of human life's basic needs: food, shelter, and clothing. More than half of all Haitians, 55 percent, live on less than $1.25 a day; seven in ten live on less than two dollars, according to a 2007 U.N. report.[1]

Johnny Henrisma and his family are under constant financial stress because he cannot find regular work, or even irregular work for that matter. In May 2006, Johnny borrowed fifty Haitian gourdes, about $1.40 U.S., to buy rice and beans for himself, his wife, and their three children and godson who were living with them. The family made these staple foods stretch into three small meals over three days, or one a day. "Tonight, we eat, and we are grateful," Johnny said to me one afternoon while Edele fixed supper. "But tomorrow, we do not know."

The same could be said about his house: tomorrow is not guaranteed. Johnny walked into his bedroom and carried out a manila envelope, smudged light gray with fingerprints. He unlatched the only prong of the clasp and pulled out some equally weathered financial papers.

Through Augustin, he began to explain in Creole to me how poor Haitians buy a house. They start with the land.

Johnny had bought the land in the mid-1990s on which he would build his family's three-bedroom house, but as of May 2006, he still owed 7,380 Haitian dollars—about 1,054 U.S. dollars. He managed to make one payment on the land because the Catholic nun from Italy who runs his children's school gave it to him. He said he owed another four thousand Haitian dollars, or about 571 U.S. dollars, by June 30. And if he did not pay, the landowner would evict him, board up the house, and lock the gate with a different lock. Then the family would be homeless.

Johnny said he spent another eighteen thousand Haitian dollars, or almost 2,600 U.S. dollars, on sheet metal, rebar, wood, nails, paint, gravel, stone, and cement mix to pour his own cinder blocks. If he were evicted, he would have no means to recoup his initial construction costs or equity.

During my third visit to his home in May 2006, Johnny asked me to help him financially. He said his greatest worry was being evicted. He said anything I could give would help.

One well-meaning American, a missionary who worked in Haiti for more than twenty years, had repeatedly warned me not to be "seduced" by Haitians. The missionary knew first-hand about how Haitians can play on an American's guilt, as Haitian co-workers had stolen from him. They can tell stories, the missionary said. And at any rate, my American friend said, direct aid to a Haitian is like spitting in the wind.

In addition to general questions of whether to give money to Haitians, I faced a second ethical dilemma as a journalist. You're not supposed to buy stories. Checkbook journalism, it's called. No currying favor with gifts. It's acceptable to buy a source a meal or a cup of coffee—that's standard business for a newspaper reporter in the United States—but gifts are another matter. But seeing families, especially younger children, go without food for a day at a time moved me to slip a ten- or twenty-dollar bill to Johnny or to Louisilia Louis.

Louisilia's brother, Oril, who goes between Gonaïves and the neighboring Dominican Republic for work, had confronted me during my second visit to that home. Oril told me that lighter-skinned, French-speaking Haitians are wealthy and take advantage of the poorer, darker-skinned Haitians. He said he had no reason to believe that a white American writer wouldn't do the same—that is, financially benefit from his relationship with defenseless people in the slum. We had sat for the interview in one of their two bedrooms, the only rooms in Louisilia's house, crowded with the entire family of children. Essentially Oril wanted to know what it was worth to me for his sister to cooperate and tell me her story.

Reflection later in the writing process revealed to me the power struggle at play in Oril's confrontational move. In the larger world order of class and race, Oril is at the bottom. Haitians are the poorest of the poor in the western hemisphere, viewed stereotypically from the outside as impoverished and desperate "boat people," beggars, and drug runners, and as violent and promiscuous, leading to one of the world's highest rates of HIV and AIDS. Between 100,000 and 140,000 people of all ages in Haiti live with HIV, according to UNICEF.[2]

There is a social hierarchy even in Haiti. The poor and darker-skinned say that 1 percent of the country's population, the lighter-skinned, French-speaking people, control half of Haiti's wealth—academically defined as those items of economic value that an individual owns. The highest 10 percent of Haitian households' rate of income or consumption is 47.7 percent, compared to 0.7 percent for the lowest 10 percent.[3] Then there is the fact of the notorious exploitation Oril experiences as a Haitian when he travels to the Dominican Republic to try to find work. He and other Haitians are considered a subclass by their neighboring nation.

So there was Oril, face to face with a white American in his home—a white American man, no less—asking for something: access to the lives and story of his family, and especially of his sister Louisilia. Of course he would want to exercise some sort of control—however temporary.

Greater thought on his confrontation later even allowed me to frame his effort as something admirable. Oril was neither passive nor a victim. He was an active agent, trying to make a way where there was almost no way to be made, seeking and winning compensation. Still, these thoughts would come to me after I returned to the United States.

On the spot, the moment was naturally uncomfortable. The rest of the family, including Louisilia, had grown silent behind Oril's lead. I excused myself with Augustin. Sweat dripped down my face and down the middle of my back. We walked outside. I took a deep breath and sighed, relieved to escape momentarily and think without Oril's intense gaze directly in my eyes.

"Money, right, he wants money?" I asked.

"Yes," Augustin said.

"Would twenty U.S. dollars be too much, not enough, insulting?"

"It would be good," Augustin said.

I had come too far with this project. I'd flown to Miami and then on to Port-au-Prince and gotten a ride to Gonaïves. I had invested money in travel and invested time visiting with and interviewing the first two families, those headed by Johnny and Fritz. (Fritz, by the way, never asked me for financial help. He just asked me to pray for his family.)

Selfishly, I thought about how I needed to move forward with the interview process with this third family.

"What will they do with the money?" I asked Augustin.

"They will buy food," he said.

The fact that the family would use the money for food allowed me to reconcile my internal conflict.

Oril stood at the door of the small house when Augustin and I walked back in. He held his baby daughter.

I had a twenty-dollar bill in my hand. I held out my hand, the money tucked in my palm, and handed it as discreetly as possible to him. He remained silent and tucked the bill into his pants pocket. He then quietly spoke into his sister's ear, and though I could not hear and would not have understood, he apparently told his sister that she could now answer my questions.

One of the questions I asked Louisilia that second afternoon was how much money it required to run her household for a year: to feed, shelter, and clothe her family. She said she spent ten thousand Haitian dollars on food and rent, not counting clothes. That's about 1,430 U.S. dollars annually for her, her sister and brother, and their combined nine children and one grandchild.

I had mostly come to terms ethically with handing out a few dollars, especially to her. My solution: I would simply disclose what I had done in the book. The reader would know. The reader could decide whether I had been ethical.

I didn't care if I was being duped. I didn't want to think that I could have prevented a family from going hungry another night but chose not to help. What would it say about me had I gained these families' trust and access to their homes, witnessing the daily struggle to acquire food, and not provided them with at least some temporary relief?

I thought of a journalism professor I had known in college at Miami University in Oxford, Ohio, in the early 1980s. His name was Hugh Morgan. I took features writing and news writing classes from him. "You're a human being first," he repeated whenever ethical discussions took place. So, more than twenty years later, in Haiti, I would be a human being first. As a journalist and writer, I would just tell readers the truth. I gave money to the heads of two of the families whose lives I documented.

My mind turned, too, to Kevin Carter. He was the white South African photographer who won the Pulitzer Prize for his March 1993 frame of a starving Sudanese toddler being stalked by a vulture. Accounts of how Carter, who later would commit suicide, captured the image are conflicted. The most widely accepted version is that the emaciated girl had stopped to rest while trying—crawling—to get to a feeding center. Carter said in interviews that he waited twenty minutes, poised with his camera, hoping the vulture would spread its wings. He said he snapped the photograph and chased the vulture off. Critics chastised him for simply taking the picture and not bothering to help the child.

There was also the matter of whether I affected, essentially changed, the lives I was attempting to document. Did I become a character in the story? I realized in the writing process that despite my attempts to stay out of the story, I was indeed a character in it.

The bigger question of whether to help Johnny Henrisma with his land payment was significantly more difficult to resolve. I made my decision before leaving Haiti late that May. I would send a check for one thousand U.S. dollars to my host, Father Gérard Dormévil, the pastor of Holy Family Church. The international courier service DHL delivered in Haiti. I asked him to cash it upon receipt and give six hundred dollars to Johnny Henrisma for his land payment. The other four hundred dollars would go to Louisilia Louis to use at her discretion. I suspected for food.

I spent hours in the homes of the three families conducting long, detailed interviews about their daily lives. I spent a day with Rosemène Cénécharles in her shop. Augustin and I spent a night in the Cénécharles house. I walked home from school with these families' children. I sat on their porches in silence during rainstorms. I attended the same Masses at church. I became part of the community. I came to know them well—and them me—and like them.

Beyond giving them some money for basic needs, I wanted to provide a meaningful gift to these families. The adults and children alike were fascinated by my simple digital camera and liked to look at what I had shot of them on the display screen.

In a package I sent along with the check to Father Gérard, I included a photo album for each family with color copies of all the pictures I had taken of them, their homes, and their belongings, some of which are in this book. Members of each of the families had told me that most of their photographs and other mementos had been destroyed or lost in storm-related flooding over the years.

I visited the families in Gonaïves again in June 2008. On that visit, I had become more comfortable giving them modest amounts of money to buy food because I had decided to reveal the truth to the readers.

Chapter 7

Work

Fritz Cénécharles has a skilled trade as a mason, yet jobs are so scarce in Haiti that he has three times gone overseas on work visas. Estimates by the U.S. government place adult unemployment in Haiti at 75 percent. Even more discomforting for him and other parents in Haiti is the grim reality that work conditions are unlikely to improve for their children.

Fritz has gone to extremes to try to find a steady job. He flew twice to the Bahamas, the first time for eleven months in 2003. He went back a year after he had returned to Haiti and stayed for twenty-one months but could not find work. He was arrested for overstaying his permit and sent back to Haiti. He left Haiti again in 2008 and returned a year later. Fritz, in his mind, has clear reasons for going overseas.

"I was obliged to leave the family, but I did not want to. I was obliged to go to try to find work. My father died. My mother is still living. They cannot help us [financially]. I have children. I am in Haiti, and I cannot find work," he said in 2006. "I decided to leave to go somewhere to try to find work and try to help my family. The children, they go to school, they need help. But I cannot afford to do that. Even if I cannot do much, I need to try to do something to help them. I had to try my best. That's why I decided to go somewhere else."

Overwhelmed by the poverty in their homeland, many Haitians look overseas for work. As of 2006, the Haitian population in the Bahamas had swelled to an estimated thirty thousand to sixty thousand, according to the International Organization for Migration (IOM). Haitians are the largest migrant community in the Bahamas and stand out because of their poor English-language abilities, impoverished living conditions, and desire for unskilled or semi-skilled jobs, the IOM said in a report by the BBC and Caribbean Media Corporation.[1]

The number of Haitian migrants, understandably, is greater in the Spanish-speaking Dominican Republic, which shares the Caribbean island of Hispaniola with Haiti. As many as 700,000 to one million Haitians are living, most illegally, in the Dominican Republic, according to a 2006 report by the *Christian Science Monitor*.[2] Desperate for work, Haitians will take the lowest-paying jobs in agriculture and construction.

Promised jobs in construction, the majority of Haitian workers, including children, end up enslaved on sugar cane plantations, according to *The Price of Sugar* (Uncommon Productions, 2007; dir. Bill Haney), a documentary film about the efforts of a Spanish Catholic priest, the Reverend Christopher Hartley, to fight for improved living conditions for the poor.

Oril Louis is one of those workers who go back and forth across the border that divides Haiti from the Dominican Republic. He has been employed from time to time in the Dominican Republic, where he also had married. His wife died in January 2006, four months before I met him at his sister Louisilia's house in Gonaïves. He has a daughter, Micheline, born in 2004. She has oversize brown eyes filled with a sad, flat stare. "Her mother was very sick. She lost a great deal of weight," Oril said to me while he held the girl.

He and his sisters, Louisilia and Dieumène—all of whom

are widowed—pool their resources. "If I have [money]," Oril said, "I share it with her [Louisilia]. I keep half. I send half back to her." He is protective of his sisters. "We have always helped each other. We learned that from our parents," Louisilia said.

Oril picked up the thought again during another interview at the Louis house: "We used to sit with our parents and talk to them. They said, 'If you have a piece of bread, you must share it with your brothers and sisters.'"

Life is difficult in the Dominican Republic for Haitians. Extreme acts of violence include the attack on four Haitian men in the capital, Santo Domingo, in August 2005. They were gagged and set afire, the *Christian Science Monitor* reported.[3] Then twenty shacks where Haitian migrants lived were set afire. Two Haitian workers were beheaded because they were believed to have been involved in the killing of a businessman from the Dominican Republic.

Haitian workers can make up to $2.50 U.S. a day in the Dominican Republic. Unemployment is roughly 17 percent, and the economic growth rate of 7 percent was one of the Caribbean's highest in 2005. Still, wages are paltry, considering the backbreaking work of cutting cane for fifteen to eighteen hours a day in tropical heat and humidity.

Haitians will send that money back to their families in their native land, similar to the practice of undocumented workers in the United States sending earnings back to their families living in Mexico, Guatemala, and other impoverished Central American nations.

At least, Oril said when our discussion turned to the plight of undocumented workers in the United States, he is able to come and go. He would not offer any detail when I pressed him to be more specific about the kind of work he does.

"Construction" is all he would say.

Some Haitian workers throughout the history of the antagonistic neighboring countries have not been as fortunate as Oril. They are kept against their will at times, confined to shanty worker villages, where there is just one water pump and little if any medical care. One Haitian worker told *Price of Sugar* filmmakers that he cut his hand to the bone with a machete, yet no antibiotics were available to him to prevent infection. Supervisors told him if he didn't work, even seriously injured, he would not be paid.

Haitian workers are the foundation of an industry in the Dominican Republic that exports 185,000 tons of sugar a year to the United States, worth some $74 million annually, according to the documentary. The practice has been in place for generations.

In 1996 in the Haitian town of Bon Repos, a few miles north of Port-au-Prince, I met Raphael Séraphim, an elderly man called "Bandito" by his fellow residents in a combination nursing home and orphanage run by a Dutch minister. Séraphim had worked all of his adult life in the Dominican Republic on a sugarcane plantation. I told his story in the *Cincinnati Enquirer* on February 4, 1996.

Séraphim was born in 1924 in the northern coast city of Cap-Haïtien. He turned twenty-one in 1945. "I could not find work," he told me through a Creole-speaking translator. "I met a man who said if I paid him fifteen dollars, he would get me work on a fishing boat in the Dominican."

Séraphim was driven across the border but dropped off inland at the plantation. He would spend the next forty-four years there, denied the opportunity to find a wife and have children. "I lived in a little house with four other people," he said. "They woke us up at three thirty every morning."

The years of swinging a machete left his hands bent and rigid and with the texture of dried leather. His back remained hunched from the constant stooping. The tropical sun cost him his eyesight. He would close his eyes during our interview, though, as if to focus on a memory. "We would work until six thirty or seven [in the morning], when we ate breakfast. Then we would be out until dinner at six. And if there was more work to do, we would not finish until ten o'clock. My hands always bled."

In 1989, when he had turned sixty-five years old, Séraphim was placed on a truck with other older cane cutters and driven back inside the Haitian border, where they were dumped. Their bodies had broken down to the point where they were no longer productive. There would be younger, stronger men available to take their place. The cycle continued.

Séraphim would be homeless and hungry for the next two years, living on the sides of roads in his homeland with no family to care for him. In 1991, he heard a radio speech by then-president Aristide that called for the Dominican Republic to return Haitian laborers to Bon Repos. Séraphim hitched a ride in the back of a truck and made his way toward Port-au-Prince. But life was no better there until the Dutch Protestant minister found him and took him in.

By the time I met him, Séraphim had lived five years in the home with some sixty other elderly people and more than two hundred orphans. It was a place with a school, church, water well, fish hatchery, and gardens, where agricultural skills were taught by growing fruits and vegetables.

"I get three meals a day. I hear the word of God. If I am sick, I see a doctor. I am treated with respect," he said. "I know God brought me to this place."

Fritz Cénécharles said he has experienced much the same sense of spiritual deliverance when returning to Haiti from the Bahamas. "Being home with [his wife and children] is like being on vacation every day," he said. "It was like a party to see her again."

The Cénécharles family survives day to day because Fritz's wife, Rosemène, is a vendor in the main Gonaïves market. She sells clothing and household items. She borrows money on a monthly basis to stay in business. There's a perception among some of their neighbors in Trou Sable that Fritz and Rosemène are better off than most.

"If you don't complain, people think you have money," Fritz said. "My wife is always working. We go to church. I come home and do something here. She is always moving. It would be best if I could find some steady work."

"When I arrived in the Bahamas, I was thinking about the children, my family," Fritz said when asked about his experience in Nassau. "It was not easy for me in the Bahamas because I was illegal. The police tried to arrest me, and I could not find work. I did not feel well the whole time I was there"

He flew there on a commuter plane. The flight cost 350 U.S. dollars, which he borrowed from a Haitian friend but had not yet been able to pay back. He had taken a bus from Gonaïves south to Port-au-Prince. His wife and children missed him. His absence hurt them emotionally.

"It was very difficult for me to see my husband leave me, but I was obliged to stay and do my work here. I am a follower of Jesus. I am a Christian," Rosemène said.

Fritz said his family of seven lives on six thousand Haitian dollars a year—roughly 860 U.S. dollars. But they are better off financially, he said, than his parents were.

"My mother had eight children. My father had ten children. There were eighteen total children," Fritz said. "My father had many wives. My father was a farmer. He was not able to take care of everyone. We were not able to finish school."

As Fritz grew up, he prayed to find one wife. "My father, having many wives, was not friendly with my mother," he said. "They did not live well together. They always argued."

As a young man, Fritz wanted to be a carpenter, bricklayer, or driver. He finished his apprenticeship as a mason in 1988. The daily life of making ends meet is difficult for Fritz and Rosemène. But they are happy. So are their children. Still, he frets about the future. Though he is a spiritual man and normally sleeps well, he said, Fritz will wake sometimes in the middle of the night. He combats his worry with Catholic prayers:

Deliver us Lord from every evil
And grant us peace in our day
In your mercy keep us free from sin
And protect us from all anxiety
As we wait in joyful hope
For the coming of our savior, Jesus Christ

"My fear is for my children," Fritz said. "I do not want to see them involved in bad situations. I do not want to see them involved in guns, to steal, or to do harm to other people. I would like each of them to have a profession, to have a job. They would not only be able to help themselves but also each other."

The chances of conditions improving for the next generation in Haiti are not good. Bleak educational and career prospects are common in Haiti. The children in these three families are unlikely to escape the impoverished conditions in which they've grown up. They know they are fortunate to even attend school. Up to 40 percent of Haitian children don't, according to a 2006 statistical analysis of Haiti by the U.S. State Department.[4] Just barely more than half of Haitian adults can read.

The fortunes of the oldest child in a family can set the tone for what happens to brothers and sisters who follow. In the three families, most of the children attend Catholic schools. Haitians value education. Often, however, one's hopes to be the exception and give back to the Haitian people simply give way to sad resignation. Malaise can take hold early—sixteen-year-old Dieunel Henrisma, for example, tries to pack his mind with math and science before time runs out, as if he's racing a clock.

Haiti is a very young country. An estimated 70 percent of the population is under age thirty, and the fifteen-to-twenty-nine demographic makes up about half of its population. Though Haiti registers some of the lowest education levels in the western hemisphere, its young people possess talent, potential, and creativity. Much of their promise is wasted because of the lack of educational and employment opportunities. Half of Haitians in their twenties don't have work.

Dieunel, the oldest of five living children in the family of Johnny and Edele, doesn't see a college scholarship on the horizon. Only 2 percent of Haitian children finish high school. Dieunel was in eighth grade at Holy Family Catholic School in the Trou Sable slum at the time of our first interview in May 2006.

Studying hard fills his time. "Every day I go to school in the morning, and I go back at night," he said.

There is electricity at Holy Family School, where a generator will power lights until nine o'clock at night. At his home, there are only a few minutes of electricity per day, most commonly in mid-afternoon.

Dieunel would like to be a doctor in order to help his family and the people in his neighborhood. Yet it's not the medical field he's likely to enter as a young man. What waits is the crippling poverty that afflicts his family. "Yes, I know, it does," said Dieunel, softly, his voice barely above a whisper.

Mackenson Cénécharles was nineteen when we met. He had finished trade school the year before in photography but could not find work either. He had re-enrolled in a Catholic high school. But he would rather be helping his parents financially. Mackenson's inability to find a job, even with a trained skill, has colored his plans for the future. He knows his family's history. He knows his father, Fritz, has gone overseas repeatedly to try to find work to support his family. He sees his mother, Rosemène, work seven days a week but knows that her small business is a fragile one financed by a series of rolling loans. He has three younger sisters and a younger brother.

"When I think of the economic situation, I would rather wait to have children," said Mackenson, who resembles his father with an even voice and tall and angular frame. "If you have a child, your parents already have suffered for you, and they will help you with your child and they will suffer again [as grandparents]."

His father commented on the implications of Mackenson marrying and starting a family. "Yes, it would be easy for him to find a woman and have a family quickly. He is very mature," Fritz said. "He has been suffering, and I would like for him not to suffer. I'd like him to wait. I always discuss that with him—always."

The eldest son has a positive example of marriage in his home. His parents have been married since October 12, 1986. Still, he knows there have been tough times.

"When they have a problem, we don't know about it,"

Mackenson said. "They sit quietly and talk about it. I don't see my parents yell at each other. I have never seen that. If it has happened, I have not seen it."

Mackenson and Dieunel appreciate that they have fathers in their lives. Many Haitian children, such as Louisilia Louis's son Prévilus Tony Cémouin, who goes by Tony, do not. Tony's stepfather, Jean-Claude Cénécharles, a former tap-tap driver, died in 2002. Tony—the oldest in his family—would like to make money to give to his mother, who has struggled just to feed, shelter, and clothe her five children. He studies by himself and with friends when he is not in school. He was sixteen and enrolled in eighth grade at a public school in 2006. He wanted to be a doctor, too.

Tony said his tear ducts have dried out. He can no longer cry. He is emotionally empty. But his three younger brothers and younger sister do cry. So does his mother. "She cries, too, because she does not have anything to feed them," Tony said.

He might not cry, but he is afraid often. Gang violence and shootings are common in his neighborhood. Thoughts and anxiety about his future become secondary to survival. "There are shootings all the time," he said. "There are guns and gangs everywhere."

Armed robbers will attack a house and leave with anything of remote value. "If I could do one thing for my country, I would stop the gang people who come to your house," he said.

He lives in what amounts to a cinder-block duplex that his widowed mother rents. The frames of the family's beds rest on concrete blocks. When the heat and humidity at night are unbearable, they will sleep under the beds on the concrete floor because it is cooler. The elevated beds also provide Tony with a sense of security.

"When there are shootings outside at night, I will hide

under the bed and get my sister and brothers to get under their bed, too," he said. "When the younger ones are not here and there are gun shots, I will go out to look for them."

Crime and health are two of the many imposing obstacles facing Haiti's youth. Dieunel Henrisma loves school, though it is not easy for him. He suffers from physical ailments for which he does not have simple medication.

"Every morning my eyes water," he said. "My vision is bad. I cannot see the blackboard very well in school. I cannot do what I want to because I have disabilities. I do not get angry. I am following my parents' faith."

School is where he is guaranteed to be fed. His family might go a day or two without food because Dieunel's father, Johnny, cannot find work. In Haiti's Catholic schools, students are fed one or two modest meals a day—rice and wheat, maybe some chicken—which they will either eat or save to take home and share.

At sixteen, Dieunel already has had two younger siblings, a brother and a sister, die of the Haitian catchall ailment, "the fever." Two of his siblings, another brother and sister, live in the country with their paternal grandmother. There are a younger brother, Nelson, and a sister, Dieuna, at home. Their only game is marbles. "We lost some of them, but we usually have enough to play," Dieunel said.

Dieunel is wise beyond his years, but he is still a teenage boy. A gifted singer himself, he likes a Haitian hip-hop singer named Top Adlerman and the song "My Problem"— "Pwoblem Mwen" in Creole. "I hear him on the radio in the house when we have electricity," Dieunel said.

He allows himself, once in a while, to think about what he might be able to do if he lived in the United States. He would get his eyes treated. He would complete his medical training and return to Gonaïves, where he would open a practice and support his mother, father, brothers, and sisters. That would be his life's work. He dreams and prays.

"With God's help, I might one day be able to be what I want to be," he said. "I know what kind of life they [his brothers and sisters] will have. I am worried. They might not be able to finish their studies or find any work."

Dieunel harbors no shame toward his parents, community, or country. He has intense love for his father and mother. He also knows that the people in his country can't get work, despite their efforts—such as Fritz going overseas.

"I am proud of my parents. My parents don't have very much. They cannot afford to do what they would like to do," Dieunel said. "I know my parents do their best every day to care for us."

Chapter 8

Flag Day

Shortly after eight o'clock in the morning on Thursday, May 18, 2006, more than one thousand Holy Family Catholic School students—dressed in uniforms of plaid skirts or blue pants with pale yellow shirts—stood in neat lines in the U-shaped compound and watched the Haitian flag being raised. It was Flag Day, a national holiday in Haiti.

Many children walking home from school the day before had carried handmade paper Haitian flags, colored red and blue with crayon and stapled to small sticks, for informal parades on Thursday. I was riding north from Port-au-Prince to Gonaïves on Wednesday and heard on the radio a discussion featuring a government official and a Haitian college professor. They were talking about the importance of young Haitians having national pride and hope in a better future for their homeland.

Their words played out before me in the demonstration in the schoolyard. I stood on the first balcony of the three-story school building and watched. Students listened first to a prayer read by two students through a megaphone. Then they turned and stood stiffly at attention. The scene unfolded with almost military precision. Students in each line policed each other into forming neat lines and showing respect. As the flag went up the pole, the students, ranging from kindergarten to twelfth grade, their teachers, and the school administrators started to sing the Haitian national anthem, "La Desalinyèn":

March on, united march, march on!
Unite for ancestors and country!

The Haitian flag, attached to a rope, rose up the pole in stops and starts as students pulled from the ground. Flag Day in Haiti commemorates the defiance of African general Jean-Jacques Dessalines, who ripped the white stripe out of the three-colored French flag and threw it into the sea. Blue and red remained. Haiti, the first destination of enslaved Africans in the western hemisphere, declared its independence on January 1, 1804, after defeating the armies of Great Britain, France, and Spain.

The school principal, a very dark-skinned Haitian man about thirty-five years old wearing a white shirt, geometrically patterned tie, khaki pants, and silver wire-rimmed glasses, spoke briefly to students through the megaphone. Then he dismissed students to their classrooms.

Later in the day, I talked with a couple of students about their nation. I simply asked how they felt about it. One high school student responded, "I would die for my country."

In turn, I was asked what I thought about the United States, my homeland. I said that I, too, loved my country, though as I grew older, in all honesty, I was less nationalistic than I had been even ten years earlier. The quote attributed to Dr. Paul Farmer, who has worked against preventable diseases in Haiti, now made perfect sense to me: "The only real nation is humanity."

I said that following the September 11 terrorist attacks in New York and Washington, D.C., in 2001, I had experienced a profound regret that I never had served in the U.S. military. Coming out of high school, I had been offered a Navy ROTC college scholarship, but I had declined at the last minute.

"My country has done much good, and I am grateful for the many opportunities I have had," I said. I remember speaking formally, measuring my words very carefully. As the minority, one feels the weight of speaking for all in his group. I knew I was coming across even more awkwardly than usual.

"But I think," I continued slowly, "we can do more good and less harm. We have so much. We are capable of much more good. We have unlimited potential. I do not know how and when fear became the primary motivation and emotion of my country. I don't know how we grew so afraid." My Haitian interpreter, Augustin, had no problem keeping up with me verbally.

There's nothing like being out of the United States for a while to make an American examine the culture back at home. I have a difficult time reconciling how much I have as a white, male American, well educated and well employed, when so many in my own country and the rest of the world have far less. And my life's experiences have shown me that the ones suffering the most do not share my skin color.

As a Christian drawn to the Catholic teaching of social justice, I believe I will be held accountable. Jesus taught that God, on our judgment day, will ask what we did to help the needy and the poor. Church law says we are to give to the poor from our own pool of resources. Salvation has to be earned.

"The moral test of any society is how it treats its most vulnerable members," reads the Catholic Church's Preferential Option for the Poor. Are Americans responsible only for other Americans? There are many people in our country who say they are not responsible for anyone but themselves. Does our society extend beyond our borders? Or does it do so only when it serves our needs?

As a younger man, early in my marriage, I was caught up on the treadmill of acquiring material possessions, some of it not by my choosing. Beginning what I hope is the second half of my life as a divorced father of three, I want to do a better job of showing my children that material wealth for the sake of itself is a ruse. It does not bring happiness or peace. Less is more. I think of the bumper sticker I see sometimes, but not frequently, in the United States: "Live simply so others may simply live," a quote widely attributed to Mahatma Gandhi. Never have those words made so much sense to me as they do when I am in Haiti. How can an American not consider that our domination of the planet's natural resources affects the rest of the world? Why can we not see ourselves more as a world citizen and less as the world's policeman?

The conversation about nationalism and love of country continued in the evening when Augustin and I walked to the homes of Fritz Cénécharles and Johnny Henrisma. They both had children enrolled at Holy Family who had participated in the flag-raising ceremony.

Despite their proud history, the poorest of Haitians are frustrated, to say the least, about their government. Economic conditions are so dire that one in eight Haitians lives abroad. Haiti remains the poorest nation in the western hemisphere. The per capita income barely exceeds seven hundred U.S. dollars a year, according to a U.N. report.[1] I asked members of the Haitian families about their attitudes toward their homeland. Their patriotism surprised me, on one level, but why shouldn't they love their country? I love mine.

"Well, we don't have a good president or government in

Haiti. The government in Haiti does not really care about us, about the poor," said Johnny, the unemployed mason who has to borrow money to feed his wife and three children. "The hardest thing," he continued later, when talking about living in poverty, "is when one of the children says they are hungry."

I asked him if he resented the riches of the United States. "No, no, I am not angry," Johnny said. "Your country is well cared for. In Haiti, one person has everything. The poor are getting poorer. And the rich are getting richer."

Edele Henrisma sat in the family's parlor, on one of the four plastic yard chairs arranged around the matching plastic garden table. "The rich in Haiti should help the poor in Haiti," she said.

At the time of my visit in 2006, Fritz Cénécharles had twice left his country for the Bahamas looking for work. (He would leave again in 2007, and I would miss him during my June 2008 visit.) The unemployment rate in Haiti is between 70 and 80 percent, according to the U.S. Agency for International Development.[2] "The country of Haiti is not well organized," Fritz said. "Haiti could be a wealthy country if we had better government."

Does he love his country? "Yes," he said, "but it is not possible for me to do anything to help my country. I do not see how I could help my country."

The concepts of nationalism and religion—our shared Catholicism and its teaching on poverty and other social issues—were topics that the Haitians enjoyed discussing. Without the distractions of television and other electronics, conversation is a valued and respected pastime among the poor, often while sitting in the relative cool of a covered porch. And without newspaper deadlines and other requirements of middle-class life filling my days, I had time to examine whatever entered my mind.

I slept in a room in a guest house and convent adjacent to Holy Family School. I was the guest of the Diocese of Gonaïves. The school was run by Sister Vincenzina, a Sister of Mercy from Florence, Italy. She was a teacher and in her eighth year in Haiti. She spoke no English but had learned Creole by living there. She previously was assigned to Burundi and Rwanda and saw the genocide there. She said she still could not speak of what she witnessed. She had devoted her life to selflessly serving and living among the world's most impoverished and disadvantaged people.

Several times during my stay I visited Holy Family classrooms. The day after Flag Day, Friday, I stood beside Augustin and Sister Vincenzina in the doorway of a room filled with elementary school students studying mathematics.

In Haiti, students commonly stand and greet visitors with a joyous welcome song, as they did on this day. While the students sang, my mind wandered. I started to think: whereas I attempt to stockpile worldly possessions and gain prestige, many Haitians fill that same personal space with a deep faith in God, warm spirit, and gentle sense of humor. Those things are all they really have. I came away wondering who actually has more wealth: was it me or these children? Not an original question, I admit, but discomforting nonetheless.

A visit to a developing nation also gives a Catholic a different perspective on the church. You see it in its most pure sense—feeding the hungry, clothing the naked, comforting the afflicted, educating the poor. It's not about building school gymnasiums or dealing with priest sexual-abuse scandals in Haiti. You meet Catholics from around the world—Italy and Ireland, Iowa and Indonesia. You truly see the universal nature of the Catholic Church. You can easily follow the beautiful rhythm and pace of the Mass, to the point where my spoken English during the Our Father at Mass blended with Creole into a single voice of thanksgiving.

I went to Mass several times a week in Haiti at the adjacent Holy Family Church. The habit fell by the wayside once I returned to Cincinnati, and I went back to my habit of making it to roughly two Masses every three Sundays.

In Haiti one Sunday, I attended the nine o'clock morning Mass for the school children. The music was sung to the accompaniment of only drums. Sister Vincenzina gave the sermon and told the children that the day's gospel called us to love one another. Love is action, not words, she said. And she discussed the life of a priest who had worked with and lived among the sick, and eventually died with them, declining his family's invitation to come home to die. She also talked about St. Maximilian Kolbe, who willingly gave his life in place of another person's.

That morning, I had awakened to contrasting images, images that upon reflection were emblematic of the struggle between doing what's right and conveniently ignoring it. First, before I fully had opened my eyes, in the predawn gray haze, I heard what I only could describe as the singing of angels. In fact, two young Haitian women were in the first stages of a lifelong commitment to become Sisters of Mercy. Both of the women were likely headed to Brazil in the next few years to begin their official formation. Each morning, at about five thirty, they would begin the day by singing morning prayers in Creole. They sang softly and sweetly, only interrupted by the crowing of roosters throughout the neighborhood. A few minutes after six o'clock, the sound of a choir and drums filled the air. Daily Mass was about to begin.

Then I opened my eyes. Directly above my head, on the inside of the mosquito netting, I saw a three-inch cockroach.

I didn't know how the cockroach got into the netting, and I didn't want to know. I slowly rolled out of bed and put on my shoes (but not before turning them over and shaking them out to make sure no other cockroach had crawled in overnight). Then I shook the netting and dislodged the cockroach, kicking it outside and into the garden. The singing had sounded like a call to act on what's best in us. The oversize cockroach, however, seemed to represent the reality of the world we live in.

In 1981, three years into his papacy, John Paul II wrote about the timeless inconsistency of hearing what we are to do and being unable to put that call into action. The pope's words—echoing what James Agee had written overnight in 1936, while sitting in an Alabama sharecropper's shanty, about the divinity of each soul—were summarized into this passage from *The Gospel of Life: On the Value and Inviolability of Human Life* (1995): "One on hand . . . there is a growing moral sensitivity, more alert to acknowledging the value and dignity of every individual as a human being, without any distinction of race, nationality, religion, political opinion or social class. On the other hand, these noble proclamations are unfortunately contradicted in practice" (pp. 31–32).

Fritz Cénécharles, an unemployed mason, built his family's home.
The kitchen stands in the foreground, May 2006.

Neighborhood children crowd the Cénécharles family photo, May 2006.

Fritz and Rosemène Cénécharles, May 2006.

Rosemène Cénécharles takes a rare break while working in her Gonaïves market shop, May 2006.

Fritz and Rosemène Cénécharles wear matching rosary rings, May 2006.

The Cénécharles family is one of the only families in their neighborhood with a well on their property. Fritz allows neighbors to enter unannounced to draw water and does not charge them, May 2006.

The Cénécharles children take off their muddy shoes before
entering the house, May 2006.

Rosena, thirteen (left), and Fritzlande Cénécharles, fifteen, wear
uniforms to their Catholic elementary school, May 2006.

Wisly Cénécharles, seven, holds his baby cousin, Davidson, May 2006.

Haitian girls will line up at the school well to wash mud from their dress shoes before going into class, May 2006.

Rosemène Cénécharles and her daughters sweep the dirt yard
each morning, May 2006.

The view from inside the kitchen Fritz Cénécharles built in his house in 2007, June 2008.

Rosena Cénécharles, fifteen, June 2008.

(Opposite) Mackenson Cénécharles, the family's eldest child, at nineteen, May 2006.

Fritz Cénécharles poses with daughters Rosena and Fritzlande,
May 2006.

Fritz Cénécharles, May 2006.

Rosemène Cénécharles, May 2006.

Chapter 9

Night

A few minutes before eight o'clock on the evening of Friday, May 26, 2006, I set out with Augustin and two of Fritz Cénécharles's daughters from Holy Family Parish to spend the night sleeping in their home. Initially, there were concerns among my hosts that Fritz and his family would suffer repercussions for having a *blan*—white person—in their home overnight. Haitians, I was told, can be jealous of each other for any advantage, perceived or real, that another might gain for associating with an American.

"I don't worry," Fritz said. "I don't care what people think."

I am the one who had asked for an overnight visit, and persisted in every conversation. The Haitian pastor at Holy Family, Father Gérard, had tried to discourage me whenever the topic came up.

"It is not the same in a home as it is here," he said of the guest house and convent inside the Holy Family wall. "There are many mosquitoes. The food and water, you might get diarrhea."

But I'd already had diarrhea and a low-grade fever for two days. I survived. I had medicine. Augustin had gotten sick, too. I shared my pills with him. We had bought clean-water pouches from a street vendor during a long walk to the

Gonaïves cemetery. The water was clean. The clear-plastic pouches were not. We had to bite the corner of the pouch to get to the water. As for mosquitoes, they were thick at the convent. And one morning I had awakened to the sight of a three-inch-long cockroach hanging directly above my head.

My only concern about the overnight stay was any trouble it might cause Fritz and his family. "My home is your home," he said, when I asked a second time if he would be affected negatively by my stay. "My door is always open."

I had soup for dinner at the convent. I did not want Fritz and Rosemène to have to prepare additional dinner for Augustin and me. We set out later than planned.

The street was dark when we walked out of the school gate. Walking at night in Haiti was a new experience for me. A dinnertime rain shower had made the streets soft and slippery. We had to negotiate past the puddles in the dark. No streetlights. No porch lights. My eyes were slow to adjust. Against the darkening gray night I saw the warmth of yellow lights—oil lamps—illuminating the cinder-block grids that are windows in some houses. I thought about the lives of the people inside. Did they eat that night? Were children's stomachs filled or aching with hunger?

Stars filled the sky. Starlight reflected in the glassy, still water of a puddle. My eyes finally adjusted.

"Blan, you are walking at night?" a woman called to me in Creole from her porch. "We never see a blan walking at night."

The four of us walked through the streets, which were less crowded at night. The air was cooler than in the light of day. I felt a sense of uneasiness, though I knew I was not in danger. Still, I felt a sense of relief when we reached Fritz's gate.

Rosemène had just returned from her market stand.

Nadège, the oldest daughter, seventeen but still in the eighth grade at Holy Family, remained at school, where she studied biology with friends in the lighted classroom—even on a Friday night. The generator ran at the school until nine o'clock every night. The oldest child, Mackenson, nineteen, was at a party at his school.

Wisly, who had just turned seven, was in bed when we arrived. He was still for the first time since I had met him the week before, but his stillness didn't last long. Within minutes, he fell out of bed. He had a dream that he was being chased by some friends. Everyone laughed, including Wisly.

I sat in a white metal chair on the main porch. Fritz and Rosemène sat in chairs. A man who lived down the street was there. Augustin sat on a bench. Wisly, out of bed and running around the yard, found his way to me and climbed onto my lap. He started to rub the hair on my head.

"Another child told me I had hair like a duck," I said to him. "Do you agree?"

"Yes," he said. Everyone laughed.

The two daughters—Fritzlande, fifteen; and Rosena, thirteen—had changed from their school uniforms. They had put on white nightgowns, which contrasted sharply with their dark brown skin. The two thin girls shared a chair across from me on the porch where their mother had been sitting and listening to a transistor radio. Rosemène would turn the volume down while changing stations. She was searching for religious music, a staple of the limited Haitian airwaves. When she found a song she liked she turned the volume back up and sang softly under her breath.

Stars dotted the black sky. The evening felt like a Friday night back in the United States. The rhythm was the same. It was time to let go of the week. There was no school the next morning.

"A good week, thanks be to God," Rosemène said when I asked how her business had gone since Monday. She would return to the market the next morning after Augustin and I left.

Fritz rose from his chair and started the white Honda motorcycle. He was headed to the school to pick up Nadège. I rubbed Wisly's back on top of his shirt. I could feel his body slump in relaxation. Soon, though, he jumped down and stood behind my chair. His attention again turned to my hair, which was cut close on the sides and in the back but a little longer on the top. It was brown, flecked with gray, and straight.

"The front needs to be cut," Wisly told Augustin. Wisly ran into his room to get a comb. His mother stopped him from running it through my hair. Then Rosemène offered us food and drink. We declined. She insisted and sent Mackenson off with a few gourdes to buy soft drinks. He had just returned from his party, followed closely by his father and sister on the motorcycle.

Throughout the evening, neighbors continued to arrive with paint buckets, filling them at the well in the front yard.

"You must find a large rock, and then you break it," Fritz said of the secret to a productive well. "Then you have good water."

A woman came in with her bucket and said hello. Then there was a teenage boy. They didn't have to ask each time. Fritz had given them permission. I commented on his kindness. He shook it off.

"Some day, if I ever need help, they will be there," he said. Fritz held the transistor radio, which was tuned still to religious music. At one point, no one spoke. The music from the radio blended with the hushed tones of a choir singing down the street. A church, Fritz said. Dogs barked. Even in the dark, with no artificial light, children played outside in the street. They seemed to be playing soccer or tag. Their laughter and shrieks spoke a universal language of happiness.

All the Cénécharles children were home for the night. Nadège, still in her pale yellow blouse and plaid skirt, dragged a chair onto the concrete porch, one step up from the dirt yard. Wisly hopped into her lap. She hugged him around the waist and pulled him to her. She whispered into his ear. He laughed. She tickled him in the ribs. He giggled. She kissed him on the left cheek. On the chair beside them, Rosena and Fritzlande still sat side by side. Rosena had smiled at me several times. She had watched Wisly play with my hair earlier. Four times, she would walk behind my chair and touch my hair, rubbing the strands between her fingers. Each time she held on a little longer.

Fritz sat on the concrete porch. He stretched his legs out into the dirt. He leaned back on his hands with his elbows locked in support. The posture was one of contentment. He was at peace. His wife was in the shower. She had filled a white Sherwin-Williams paint bucket with well water and carried it toward the back corner of the property. The family had an enclosed shower made of cinder blocks, stone, and concrete. There is no running water and no hot water in most Haitian homes. People wet their bodies with the cold water. Then they wash. Then they rinse off by dumping the water over themselves.

"Tonight is like many nights," Fritz said. "We sit on the porch. We talk. We listen to the radio. We pray. Then we go to bed."

Technology and electricity do not allow family members to go in their own direction. They either go to bed or sit on the porch with their parents. There is a routine, an order, despite the seeming chaos all around them. The body clock is in sync with the sun.

Fritz secured the gate with a padlock. Rosena brought in shoes and socks that had been left on the porch or in the yard.

An oil lantern was lit. Fritz carried it from room to room. Rosemène called out instructions. Augustin and I were given Fritz and Rosemène's bed. A paint bucket was filled with an inch or two of water. It was placed at the end of our bed in case we needed to urinate during the night. The family met in the salon for prayers. The lamp rested on a coffee table.

Rosemène led family prayer with her rosary ring. She and Fritz each wear one. She sang the prayers. Her husband and children followed in response. Wife and husband sat on the couch. The children were piled around them on chairs or the floor. Wisly and Rosena, the two youngest children, fell asleep, Wisly wedged between his parents on the couch. Mackenson and Nadège, the two oldest, looked at each other silently, rolling their eyes, when prayer time appeared to be lasting longer than normal. After thirty minutes, the prayer session ended. Everyone went to bed.

Wearing just a pair of running shorts but no shirt, I eased into the queen-size bed. I rested on a white sheet. The bed-spread had been pulled off, folded, and placed on a dresser. I tried to sleep on my stomach. It was too hot. Sleeping on your back is most comfortable and coolest. I've learned in Haiti just how much heat is produced by the internal organs on the front of the body.

Fritz and Rosemène had pushed the coffee table aside in the salon and spread a thin, padded mat on the smooth concrete floor. The oil lamp, which had thrown a shaft of light through the doorway, was extinguished. They said they didn't mind sleeping on the floor. It was cooler than the bed.

I drifted in and out of light sleep. In the distance, I heard dogs bark. One bark on my left seemed answered by a bark from another dog on my right. I heard a radio: soft ballads, the midnight soundtrack of lovers.

I heard Fritz's deep breathing. Rosemène sang a soft hymn deep into the night. My thoughts turned to Fritz and his wife on the floor, and to my own situation. I am divorced, broken, anxious, sad, and lonely at times. My eighteen-year marriage had ended a year earlier. The depth of my guilt, failure, and sense of loss would not hit me fully for more than two years.

Man clings to wife in the night. The presence of her being calms his fears. He sleeps, wrapped in her strength. I imagined Fritz and Rosemène together on the floor: Fritz on his side, his arm slid beneath his wife's pillow and neck; Rosemène clasping his wrist or perhaps interlocking her fingers with his. His arm reached across the curve of her hip. Despite the humidity and oppressive heat, she slid her back into his chest. They lost the concept—physically and emotionally—of where his body ended and hers began. They merged into one. Time stopped, even as the minutes raced toward daylight. Did he notice if his breathing pattern was in rhythm with hers, or off by half a beat?

There in the dark, I ached to find a woman to hold, to comfort and to be comforted by. Fritz had won where I had lost. His marriage had lasted. Mine had ended.

In the other room, Wisly groaned and sniffed in his sleep.

The dark night in a home with no electricity was almost akin to serving a jail sentence. There was no chance to read. I could not get up and turn on a radio or television or listen to music. There was nowhere to hide from thoughts of mortality, of how I live and the decisions I've made. I considered the differences in our lifestyles, Americans and Haitians. I have been given so much, hundreds of daily conveniences that Fritz, Rosemène, and their family cannot imagine—a hot shower, morning coffee, food everywhere, money, medical care, and a job. Yet I am nowhere near as faithful to God as my hosts. These thoughts were as oppressive and uncomfortable as the heat and humidity.

Roosters crowed off in the dark distance. I kept looking for daylight. It took hours to arrive. Finally, Rosemène got out of her makeshift bed, followed by Fritz. I heard her outside in her kitchen, preparing rice. She then started washing clothes in the yard. She drew water from the well. Two daughters unlocked the gate and walked to Mass at Holy Family. Nadège was sent by her mother to work the morning as a vendor at her market boutique. Rosemène would go in a couple of hours later.

The night ends. Another day begins. Members of this family take the order and security of their house as their strength against the uncertainty waiting outside of their walls.

For them, the morning brings another day of tasks, the uphill battles that are their lives.

For me, the morning brings relief.

Chapter 10

Clothing

The charcoal-colored dirt that is the front yard has been swept clean of any garbage by the time the sun comes up on a Monday morning. Another week has arrived for the Cénécharles household. Fritz Cénécharles is making sure the youngest children are ready for school. Rosemène is getting dressed for work at her clothing booth.

The four oldest children leave for school early. Only the youngest child, Wisly, seven years old, stays longer at home with his father. The daughters attend two different Catholic schools, and all three are in uniform. The common denominator is their feet. They wear black leather shoes with delicate white ankle socks. The socks fold over, revealing a lace edge and matching ribbons on the outside of each foot. The girls walk through dusty streets, marked with puddles of left-over rain or streaked pools of animal urine, yet the shoes remain pristine. If the shoes become soiled in any way, the girls will line up at a water pump in the school yard to rinse them off before heading to class.

Fritz helps Wisly get ready. He has poked an additional hole in Wisly's oversize belt so it fits the thin boy's waist. Fritz loops the remaining foot of leather belt through loops all the way to the boy's back. The pale yellow shirt is tucked into the olive-colored dress shorts. Fritz goes over Wisly's close-cropped hair with a yellow brush. The boy lifts his backpack to his shoulders and runs out the gate.

Rosemène is dressed for work. She has put on a pale green T-shirt with a lighter green skirt patterned with faint leaves. On her head she wraps a blue *mauchwa*, a small handkerchief with green and blue flowers. She rubs perfume on her wrists and the sides of her neck before leaving the house for the forty-minute walk to the market.

In the two weeks I know Rosemène, her facial features soften. Initially, I saw what appeared to be a larger, harder woman. She shows more warmth to me as the days pass. She has a broad nose and the look of a chameleon, able to change. At times she will look older to me. Then I see a girl. She will smile sometimes. But there is always a pleasant, approachable look on her face.

On her left index finger, two down from her gold wedding band, Rosemène wears a silver ring with small beads that represent one decade of the Catholic rosary. Fritz wears a matching rosary on his left index finger.

"I leave home at seven in the morning, and I come back at seven at night," she told me. "My husband stays with the children. I used to have someone to come here and watch them, but they do not come anymore. When he needs to go out, [Fritz] locks the gate. When the children come back from school, he makes sure he is here."

She walks with purpose and pride from the house in Trou Sable to Gonaïves. She carries with her plastic bags and the family's portable radio.

She has been a vendor since 1980, when she was four-teen years old. Her current outdoor shop is on Liberty Street, which is paved, a rarity in the Gonaïves area. Rosemène rents a space on the steps of a hardware store. She sells clothing and household items. She stores her stock in a closet at a friend's home near the market. The friend has lighter skin and says that she, like me, is a *blan*.

Rosemène did not learn her business skills in school. Creatively, she scratches out a living that supports her, her husband, and their five children. Her consistent presence as a merchant for many years has yielded a small but loyal customer base that trusts her.

At the friend's house where Rosemène stores her stock, she picks carefully through the large closet. It is in the courtyard of the woman's home. Rosemène carries four bamboo baskets and her stock for the day from her storeroom. She walks about a half a block, through an intersection at the middle of which a fire of garbage and old tires burns.

Rosemène borrowed ten thousand Haitian dollars (about 1,500 U.S. dollars) to start her business. She sells sheets (in their original packaging), tablecloths, towels, curtains, bandannas, pants, shirts, and personal care items such as toothpaste and hair products. Her shop is a mix of Walgreens, Bed, Bath & Beyond, and a Salvation Army thrift store.

Many Haitians, especially the poor, wear used American clothing that still carries the informal moniker "Kennedy clothes," in reference to the U.S. president who first started shipping tons of it to Haiti in the early 1960s. Merchants from outside the capital, like Rosemène, buy used imported clothing in Port-au-Prince and resell it in their hometowns. The clothing and other imported items are also called *pepe*, a common Creole term describing used foreign merchandise sold at prices Haitians can afford.

Haitians' use of discarded clothing and household items from the United States is the subject of the short documentary film *Secondhand* (*Pepe*) (Fabrik Films, 2006). In it, filmmakers Hanna Rose and Vanessa Bertozzi trace the history of used American clothing, from the high demand at home during the Depression to the glutted domestic market after World War II. Third-world countries, such as Haiti, just six hundred miles from Florida, made deals with thrift merchants in the United States for the excess clothing. Americans get rid of an estimated 2.5 billion pounds of textiles a year, and as much as 80 percent of the waste finds its way to third-world markets such as Haiti. A used boy's T-shirt from the United States is sold for as little as thirteen U.S. cents in Haiti.

Commemorative Super Bowl T-shirts printed in advance of NFL championship games—for immediate on-field display and sale afterward to fans—also end up in Haiti. T-shirts and baseball caps emblazoned with winning logos of the 2007 New England Patriots are popular there; of course, the Patriots lost.

After arriving at her spot near the Gonaïves Catholic cathedral, Rosemène sets up shop. The process takes her between twenty and thirty minutes and is one she has repeated hundreds, if not thousands, of times. She starts by placing two large rocks in the gutter where the paved street descends to meet the curb. She positions a large wooden box on the rocks and first concrete step, adjusting one of the rocks to level the box. On the box, she rests the bamboo baskets, which form a rim that is about six inches wide. Sheets and towels are stacked neatly on this edge. In the recess of the baskets she will arrange items such as hair spray, baby powder, Niagara brand starch, and stick deodorant.

She hangs bandannas in a spectrum of colors from a post that supports the roof covering the main sidewalk in front of the hardware store. Her elevated chair backs into the post. To her immediate left rest her baskets of products. Rosemène makes two quick sales—a package of sheets and a tube of toothpaste—to women she calls by name. She rearranges the items in the baskets to pass time. Several times during our stay in the market she offers to buy Augustin and me a drink of water or soda. She also made sure we had clean water the first time we went to her home.

Rosemène's modest success as a business owner has allowed her and her husband and children to live a relatively comfortable life. They have a home. They have their own well. Their children attend school. They have a motorcycle, albeit one in need of constant repair. They can feed their family every day. Still, their existence is perilous.

Rosemène's business is based on a constant flow of borrowing money and paying it back. She borrows one sum of money each year and makes twelve monthly payments to pay off the loan. The family has no money saved.

"Every month, I have to pay back. God always helps me pay back every month," she said.

At her booth, Rosemène pulls a brown apron over her skirt and ties it in the back. She wears sandals. Next to her is another booth where a man sells large bags of U.S.-produced rice and cooking oil in plastic jugs. On the sidewalk, a boy pulls a homemade toy car on a string. It is an empty white can of Shell motor oil, through which a plastic axle has been poked and a third wheel placed on the front.

She will make up to ten sales on a good day, at least five most days. But it's enough to support the family, she says. Her husband stays at home to run the household and tries to find work. Rosemène has a cell phone for which she buys minutes. So does Fritz. He will call once a day to check on her.

"He watches the children. He cleans the house. He does laundry and cooks. He irons," Rosemène said of Fritz.

Rosemène makes three sales in the next hour—a bandanna, a pair of men's shorts, and three disposable baby diapers. Diapers are sold individually, not in a pack; packs are too expensive. The men's shorts have become a consistent seller. She sells them for fifteen Haitian dollars, about two U.S. dollars.

As the minutes turn to hours, the vendors will help each other. A woman with a stand on the other side of Rosemène's needs to leave for a few minutes; Rosemène watches her stand and even makes a sale for her, even though Rosemène sells the same brand of toothpaste from the Dominican Republic.

"We need each other. We help each other. We get along very well," Rosemène said.

Late in the morning, not having eaten breakfast, Rosemène will buy two small pieces of pie from a nearby vendor. She gives one to a friend with a stand nearby. Rosemène refuses money. She lives by a Creole proverb:

Byenfe ka rann byenfe.
One kindness leads to another kindness.

The children walk home from school shortly after one o'clock in the afternoon. The school day in Haiti often begins at seven in the morning and ends at one to help avoid the day's most oppressive heat. It is mid-afternoon. The sun beats down. There is precious little shade to provide protection from the tropical rays.

Inside the walls of the Cénécharles home, fifteen-year-old Fritzlande has changed out of her school uniform into shorts and a T-shirt. She is in the kitchen, where she is beginning the early preparations for dinner: corn, fish, and tomatoes. Rosena, age twelve, is sitting in a metal chair in the shade of the front porch, where she is studying Haitian history from a workbook.

At the market on Liberty Street, Rosemène makes another sale, a pair of used white dress shoes for a girl. Rosemène's younger sister, she says, has a shop nearby. She sells many of the same types of products. A man comes by and picks through a stack of washcloths for bathing. He does not like the yellow ones that Rosemène has in stock. She tells him that her sister has green ones and points down the street to the other stand. The man walks to the other stand. He buys the green one.

Chapter 11

Returning

Daily life became noticeably more difficult in Gonaïves and in all of Haiti in the two years between my visits. I arrived back in the northern city of 200,000 people on June 26, 2008, with Augustin, following a three-hour, sixty-mile ride from Port-au-Prince on the national highway. It is a two-lane road, both paved and unpaved, deeply rutted from having been washed out by floods in 2004. (Additional flooding from tropical storms would destroy more of the road in September 2008.) There are no centerlines or other markings. Drivers steer onto both sides to avoid potholes and other jarring recesses, regardless of whether they are behind the wheel of a private vehicle or the old American school bus that is used for public transportation and is so overcrowded people are forced to sit on the roof with their possessions.

We pulled into the Holy Family gates well before eleven o'clock in the morning; its paved yard had corroded greatly in just two years. The surface was chipped with large flakes of brittle, sandy concrete loose under foot. The red and yellow paint marking the free-throw lines and boundaries of the basketball court were barely visible. No one had played here in a long while. Two years earlier this basketball court had been an important place of common ground, where I played three-on-three pickup games and the shooting game "horse"—or "chwal," in Creole—with school maintenance workers, teachers, and older students. I didn't shoot the ball too much during games. I tried to pass first and set picks so my new teammates could get the easy shots at the basket. We communicated nonverbally, pointing or directing each other with nods of our heads. We congratulated each other with handshakes, high-fives, and hugs after the game. People watched from the exterior balconies of the school. "The blan plays basketball."

If you play basketball long enough, you know inherently when someone wants badly to beat you. I knew I got the Haitians' best game. The picks were physical. They jumped high to try to block my shots. Augustin didn't want to play. He said he preferred to watch. I didn't have sneakers with me. I wore old hiking boots or beat-up Top-Sider boat shoes with no socks. I remember just being glad I didn't twist or, worse, sprain an ankle.

Two years later, the nets on the rusting basketball hoops were torn and frayed. The school building itself, three stories with exterior balconies, looked tired. The yellow and pink paint on the exterior cinder-block walls had faded almost to white. Wooden doors to the classrooms had warped and no longer hung square with the frames.

The aging process for buildings, like people, is accelerated in Haiti.

We were met in the school yard by the oldest of the Henrisma children, Dieunel, who had turned eighteen and completed tenth grade. He had grown taller and, like everyone I would see again for the first time in two years, thinner—much thinner. No baby fat left on him—not that there had been any to begin with. Food, already in short supply and costly, had become scarce and almost prohibitively expensive.

Dieunel wore a white T-shirt, blue jeans, and plain white

sneakers. He carefully sidestepped puddles in the dirt streets. The young man said little. Through Augustin, I asked if he was still in school.

"Wi," he said.

Did he still want to study medicine and become a doctor?

"Wi," he said again.

The route to his parents' home, the sights, sounds, and smells—charcoal burning, animal feces and urine, clucking chickens, snorting pigs, barking dogs, the blue paint on lottery booths—were comfortably familiar. I was less apprehensive to make eye contact or attempt to say hello in Creole to those people who walked past.

"Koman ou ye?" (How are you?)

"Tre byen, mesi." (Very well, thank you.)

Or "Pa pi mal." (Not bad.)

For all of the familiarity, there was change too. The next night, I would walk the loop from the school to the three families' homes. I would be surprised—almost startled—by what I saw in the streets. More Haitians, anecdotally and statistically, had cellular telephones in 2008 than two years before. My walks through the streets of Trou Sable after dark revealed the soft blue glow of cell phones against faces. In an unlit neighborhood where most families used oil lanterns to light their homes, people with cell phones used them almost as flashlights in the streets. Dozens of these blue lights danced in view down a long, dark straight street without any bends.

The proliferation of cell phones had given rise to a new cottage industry: someone with an electric generator would sell time on a power strip for people to recharge their phones. Churches and schools, public buildings with generators, were popular sites of phone recharging. No live outlet was left unplugged.

Rosemène and Fritz Cénécharles each have a cell phone. Overseas looking for work for the third time, Fritz would call his wife and update her on his location, report any successes or failures, and give instructions to his oldest child, Mackenson, who was the man of the house in his father's temporary absence.

The Haitian market was flooded with relatively inexpensive cell phones by a Jamaican company, Digicel, created in 2001. Digicel opened operations in Haiti in May 2006 and had two million customers in two years, making Haiti its largest consumer base, according to the company. Digicel also had two million subscribers in Jamaica. Prior to Digicel's entrance into the Haitian market, 5 percent of the population had cell phones; now the number had jumped to more than 30 percent. Landline telephones were rarely if ever seen in the homes of the poor. Haitians with Digicel phones say the phones cost them less than 250 Haitian dollars, or around thirty to thirty-five U.S. dollars. People buy phone minutes on cards from vendors in the markets. A used phone card given to me by one of the children in Trou Sable showed a black woman sitting on a cream-colored couch, smiling at her cell phone.

"Carte Flex 50 gdes," it read. As of July 2008, one Haitian gourde was worth about two and a half U.S. cents. So this used phone card was worth about $1.25 U.S. The question is obvious: why do people unable to afford food for days at a time spend money on cellular telephones?

I thought as I walked about a story I had written in 1999 for the *Cincinnati Enquirer*. It focused on the life of a married man with two daughters whose family had no private medical insurance. He worked forty hours a week as a supervisor of a small crew for a company that repaired water damage and sealed basements. Over the course of several months of reporting, I went to work with him a few times. I spent time in his home. I accompanied his family to the grocery store. I treated them to pizza, the cost of which I put on my company expense account. In his family's apartment, in the predominantly white, urban Appalachian town of Norwood, Ohio, he had a large color TV and cable access with multiple channels, including the HBO and Showtime movie networks. My assigning editor wanted to remove that detail from the story because it made the man a less sympathetic character, he said. A copy editor entered the discussion. He said he had been in the homes of migrant farm workers in California's Central Valley—houses at times with dirt floors—and they had color televisions rigged with cable, too.

I remembered the response of the working poor man when I asked him about the cost of his cable service. "I got to have something," he said. "It's the only thing I got." Television kept him connected to the larger world, access he otherwise thought he did not have.

We kept the detail in the newspaper story. My argument: it was true. Let the reader decide whether it was positive or negative.

I wouldn't bother the Haitian families that had cell phones with the same question. I'm sure the answer would have been roughly the same. They had to have something. A cell phone kept them connected to the larger world, one painfully outside of their reach of which they are increasingly aware—largely because of Internet access students like Dieunel have in Catholic and other religious schools.

Dieunel, Augustin, and I walked on, through the hot, dusty streets, the noontime sun beating down, and approached a T in the road that I recognized. The cross street ran parallel to an open sewer line. On our left, as we approached the gulley, stood Edele Henrisma, who also had lost a significant

amount of weight in two years. She laughed, almost squeal-
ing happily, when she saw Augustin and me. She hugged us
both, an embrace less reserved than I had received from her
two years earlier.

I had thought often of these three families during my time
back in Cincinnati. I read Haitian Creole poetry as part of
my reporting and writing process. The words of poet Claude
Innocent's "The Poor Man's Life" summarized what I had
seen and—in a timeless fashion—foreshadowed what I was
coming back to in Gonaïves:

Walking around looking for life
The poor man's feet lose their creases

The feet of poor Haitians had fewer creases in 2008 than
in 2006. Their mouths were drier. And their stomachs were
emptier.

We walked a narrow path to Edele and Johnny's home,
striding two abreast—Augustin beside Edele, Dieunel next to
me—squeezing between cinder-block and sheet-metal walls
and fences made of bamboo and rusted wire.

At the same time that we approached the Henrisma
house, neighbors and friends had gathered nearby at the
home of Fritz and Rosemène Cénécharles. The purpose was
to pray for Fritzlande, one of Rosemène and Fritz's teenage
daughters. Johnny Henrisma was there, and had taken his
daughter Dieuna and son Nelson with him. Rosemène was
home for the service. Nadège, nineteen years old and the
family's oldest daughter, ran the shop in the marketplace.

"She was attacked by a bad spirit," Rosemène said later
that afternoon when Augustin and I visited her home. "When
she is sick, she cannot speak.'

Foreign aid workers would later tell me, respectfully, that

it was not a bad spirit that was making her sick; she didn't have food. The girl suffered from acute malnutrition.

In Haiti, where 80 percent of the population is Roman Catholic, voodoo is widely practiced, often in a blend of the two religions. Voodoo—or *vodou*, in French and Creole—is as old as Haiti itself. The religious practices were brought to the Caribbean by enslaved people from West African nations in the sixteenth century. Slaves created voodoo by merging their traditional beliefs and ceremonies with those of their French captors. In voodoo there is one main god, Bondye, similar to the beliefs of Christianity, Islam, and Judaism. A center point of voodoo is healing people from illness with herbs and the intercession of lesser gods to Bondye, known as Loa.

In his book *Voodoo in Haiti* (1972), Alfred Métraux detailed the uniquely Haitian experience of this religious and spiritual practice. Métraux, a European-born anthropologist, summarized what he had learned in a 1961 interview that was quoted in the book's introduction. He called Haitian voodoo a "conglomeration of elements of all kinds, dominated by African tradition" and said that 90 percent of Haitians believed and followed its traditions. "At the same time," Métraux said, "these people consider themselves Catholic, and while I affirm that nine-tenths of the population practice [voodoo], I do not mean that they are not Christian. All [voodoo] believers are in effect excellent Catholics, extremely pious." In an example of this mixture of beliefs, the Haitian people in the Trou Sable neighborhood of Gonaïves prayed to drive the evil spirit out of Fritzlande.

In the early nineteenth century, Haitians kicked out most white people, including European Catholic priests, once they won their independence. Expelling priests provoked the Vatican to sever relations with Haiti for more than fifty years, and the association remained chilled into the 1950s, when

Rome finally ruled to allow voodoo drums and melodies into
Catholic Masses. I did not see any voodoo dolls or pin-sticking
ceremonies in Haiti. In fact, what I'd started to learn about
voodoo's specific religious practices and traditions made a lot
of sense to me.

I've experienced the voodoo incorporation of drums
at Masses in Haiti. Most of the Mass prayers are sung by
the congregation; there are very few spoken words. I also
attended a voodoo baptism in Port-au-Prince in 1996; a
neighbor living near the Hands Together headquarters had
invited me. The infant, wrapped in a blanket, was placed on
a dirt floor at the center of a round, wooden building, next to
the support pole. The faithful danced in an elaborate pattern
around the infant, increasing their foot speed and weaving
intricately in and out of each other's paths until I feared they
would bump into each other or, worse, accidentally kick the
child. No one did. The temperature and humidity in the room
rose to extremely uncomfortable levels. The drums beat more
loudly and faster, reaching a crescendo that made the small
space blur in sound and sight.

The marriage of the two faith traditions is so harmonious
these days, and so normal to Haitians, that for me to even ask
about the side-by-side practice of Catholicism and voodoo
would be thought of as odd. My time in Haiti and immersion
into its culture moved me to further question and view negatively the human divisions created by religious faiths and the
sometimes squabbling subsets of Christianity. I'd begun to
ask, uncomfortably at first, isn't it just about one God and the
responsibility of the haves in this world to care for the have-
nots? The label doesn't matter.

Case in point: Johnny, a fervent Catholic, spoke at the voodoo service for Fritzlande. He spoke as a voodoo priest would:
he said an evil spirit had attacked the girl. Yet he looked like

a circuit-riding Christian preacher from the American South. He carried his Bible and wore black hip-wader boots over his blue jeans. Heavy rain had fallen the day before and turned the charcoal-colored streets to slick mud at best and deep puddles of contaminated water at worst. Johnny used a white megaphone to address the group, which had assembled and prayed in the front yard of the Cénécharles home. When Johnny returned to his own house with the megaphone he removed its four D batteries to conserve their power.

Prayerful people with little in this world leaned even more heavily on prayer. "It's more important than ever; times are hard," Johnny said. "Everyone wants to have a service."

I had only been back in the country for one day, and I already was experiencing internal conflict. I ached compassionately for my Haitian friends; I didn't want them or anyone to suffer further. Yet the clear changes in their lives due to the food crisis would make for good material, one that showed physical shifts and movement. Desperate living conditions worsened still.

Personally, I had wanted to show my respect to the families by going back to Haiti. I wanted to physically see them again. Yet coming back was a greater challenge than the longer visit in 2006; I knew better what to expect. I knew the aftereffects would be physical and intellectual fatigue, a week's worth of stomach pain, and ceaseless emotional discomfort associated with my lifestyle compared to that of the people I knew well in Haiti. There was a lot of white American and Catholic guilt that I wanted, once and for all, to face and overcome in an attempt to move to healthier emotional and intellectual places.

No denying, though, I was a reporter documenting these people's lives. Many of my questions were answered swiftly.

How had the members of the families aged? How had their lives changed? Did they still live in the same houses? Had a member of a family died or survived serious illness? Had any of the older children married? Had any of the children graduated in school? Had anyone found steady work?

Of course, I was well aware beforehand of the global food crisis and how it would force the Haitians to further stretch already strained resources. When would they reach a breaking point? How much hardship could a group of people endure?

There had been food-related riots in April 2008, including one in their neighborhood, two months prior to my return visit. Understandably, food would be our first topic of conversation once we started to talk in Edele's parlor.

Chapter 12

Food

The Henrisma family would frequently go a day without food in 2006. The children, at least, would eat a meal at school when it was in session. Three pails of rice would cost 250 Haitian gourdes—or about seven U.S. dollars back then. In 2008, those would look like the halcyon days. The same amount of rice was twice as expensive.

Edele Henrisma sat in the green plastic lawn chair in the parlor of her three-room house. The four chairs were still arranged in the shape of a cross around the small, square table that came in a set, just as they had been in 2006. I sat across from Edele. Augustin was at my right. Dieunel was to my left.

There was no food in the house, Edele said. I had read reports in previous months about food-related riots in Haiti. Knowing these families by name, face, and place made the violence feel closer to home. Food prices had climbed globally by an average of 40 percent from the middle of 2007 to May 2008, the Associated Press had reported. Riots were especially violent in the southern Haitian city of Les Cayes, a major seaport, where five people were killed; Cap Haïtien, in the north; St. Marc; and Port-au-Prince, the capital, where bands of young men set up roadblocks, burned tires, and looted stores. President René Préval ordered protesters to stop and urged lawmakers in Haiti to cut taxes on food imports. The problem, Préval said in a national radio and television address, was the nation's dependence on imported rice. The prices of fruit and beans had doubled, too, and the soaring cost of food led to the dismissal of prime minister Jacques Alexis.

Rice is the staple of most Haitians' diet. Seven in ten people in Haiti live on less than two U.S. dollars a day. India and Vietnam had banned exports of rice in spring 2008; Australia's rice crop was down 98 percent because of a six-year drought, according to *U.S. News and World Report*.[1]

In Haiti, Gonaïves would be hit hard again in late August and September 2008 by three hurricanes and a tropical storm within a thirty-day span. Four years earlier, heavy rains from Hurricane Jeanne caused more than two thousand deaths in Gonaïves and the surrounding area. These successive massive floods destroyed rice crops in the fertile Artibonite region of Haiti, of which Gonaïves in the capital.

The convergence of catastrophic events crippled Gonaïves, where high school students from poor families in the slum neighborhood of Raboteau rioted and marched en masse to Holy Family School in adjacent Trou Sable, looking for more students to join the protest. When student leaders at Holy Family decided to stay in school, the marchers threw rocks at the building before moving on, Edele said. Dieunel attends Holy Family and told his parents about the altercation.

A week before I visited, Edele told me, she sold two of her dresses to buy food. "They told me they were hungry. I had to do something," she said of her children. Edele will buy as much rice as possible. "It's not enough, it's not even enough," she said. "Sometimes we now go two days—we spend two days without food. This is the reason we go to church, to pray to God to give us food."

The effects of the high cost of food were easily seen and heard. People were excruciatingly thin, emaciated. There was less food on sale in the market. People bought less. More children begged. Rosemène Cénécharles told me later that afternoon that her clothing and household items were not moving. Every sale she might make at her booth affected her ability to feed her family.

"I feed the children every day," she said, "even if it is a little flour."

Rosemène was significantly thinner than two years ago when I met her. Her children also had grown even slimmer on their already lean frames. Two of Rosemène's major top teeth were rotting. There was no money for even emergency dental work.

Fritz, who had twice previously searched unsuccessfully for work in the Bahamas, was in the southern Caribbean island nation of Curaçao, off the north coast of Venezuela.

"Life is expensive here," Rosemène said when I asked why Fritz had left. "Education is expensive here. He had to go."

Johnny Henrisma stays in Gonaïves. Like Fritz, he is a mason unable to get any steady work. At best, he can find a couple of odd jobs a month, maybe a day or two of work. His entire family, he said, had been ill with "the fever." Dieuna, who had turned eight in 2008, was especially sick. The family could not recall having vomited more violently. The scarcity of food and lack of safe drinking water were adversely affecting the health of most Haitians.

"When we don't have any food," Edele said, "we give the children a piece of salt. They put it on their tongue and let it sit there for a while. Then they take a drink of water." The idea is to create the sensation of being full.

"Physically and mentally," Johnny said when I asked how the lack of food affects them. "We are weaker. And the children always have headaches because they do not eat."

Louisilia Louis's extended family had eaten one meal on Sunday and another on Wednesday. It was now Friday. Even on a good day, when the family managed to find food, it was limited to one meal. There was no such thing as breakfast or lunch in this house.

On Friday, though, Louisilia and her family would eat. She told me on my first visit with her during my 2008 trip that they had not eaten for two days. When the interview finished, I asked her and Augustin to walk outside with me. I handed her a twenty-dollar bill. I thought back to the decision I had made in 2006 to try to help these families with money for food and, in Johnny and Edele's case, their mortgage. I decided, just as I had then, that I would simply tell the readers what I had done. They could decide whether it was right or wrong.

What I saw unfold at Louisilia's house that afternoon surprised me. The simplest meal became reason for celebration. Louisilia set out on foot with her sister, Dieumène, and the oldest of Louisilia's five children, Tony, born in 1990.

Louisilia's house was not far from the main Trou Sable market, which was near Holy Family Church. The market is a series of outdoor booths, tables, crude wooden frames, and blankets spread out along both sides of the narrow dirt street. Because of heavy daily foot traffic, motorbikes, and the occasional SUV or pickup, the street—colored gray from charcoal—is rutted. Storm water will stand stagnant. Still, merchants always set up their wares. Women sat perched behind large stainless steel bowls filled with rice. Cut pieces of chicken, mostly legs, were arranged in rows—almost baking and covered with flies—on elevated pieces of cardboard that had been folded to form tabletops. Whole fish, dead, lying on their side with one eye staring up at the sky, were lined on corrugated sheet metal. Other vendors had bowls filled with yams, small tomatoes, onions, leeks, tiny heads of lettuce, and beets, all segregated in their own areas of the container. Beans—black, white, and red, as well as the larger light brown Miami bean—were available in different bowls and cloth bags. Charcoal was available in rusted coffee cans for about sixty U.S. cents. Charcoal, made from wood burned with sand, is the primary cooking fuel for the poor and a primary reason for two environmental challenges in Haiti, widespread deforestation and poor air quality.

Still more vendors specialized in household and personal care items, such as toothpaste, soap, and shampoo, all arranged by size and color of the packages on tables or in oversize bamboo bowls. Soft drinks, including Coca-Cola and Sprite in sixteen-ounce glass bottles, some dating to 1994, were available for about fifty U.S. cents; most were sold warm. Twelve-ounce stubby bottles of Haitian-brewed Prestige beer also could be purchased, again usually without the benefit of refrigeration.

Louisilia and her sister walked past the beverage booths to the food. Their first stop was the rice, where the female vendor scooped three pails into a brown plastic bag; Louisilia asked for a double bag, so as not to loose any of the valuable commodity should one bag split open.

Just then, a rusted blue Toyota pickup steered through the mud to a high spot in the road, where the dirt was dry. The bed of the pickup was filled with mangoes, grown just out-side of Gonaïves and brought into the market. Fruit vendors walked briskly or ran to the pickup to bid on the fresh fruit. A man stood in the bed, collecting money and handing out bags of mangoes. Louisilia ignored the commotion at the pickup. At booths back down the street toward her house, she bought a bag of black beans, four chicken legs, a small measure of sugar, a couple of mangoes, and a few handfuls of tomatoes, onions, and beets. The sisters looked at fish but decided it was too expensive. The final selection was a plastic bag filled with charcoal; Louisilia bent over the pile to pick out the big-gest pieces that looked like they would burn best.

Back at home, meal preparation would involve many hands but still required at least two hours. Louisilia and one of the teenage girls carried a rusted metal stove from the sheet-metal kitchen and placed it near the cinder-block outer wall in the yard. Two other girls sat in small chairs close to the ground and poured the bag of black beans into a flat bamboo bowl. They picked up handfuls of beans and sifted out the stones and other debris. At the stove—nothing more than a metal frame with three small baskets across the top that hold charcoal—Dieumène placed the briquettes into one of the burners. A girl brought out a kerosene lantern from the house, but it was out of fuel. They lit the charcoal with a burning piece of paper. A couple of scraps of smoldering paper blew across the yard. In a few seconds, despite the breeze, the charcoal burned, filling the yard with the same odor as the street.

Louisilia poured the rice into another flat bamboo bowl. The water pump in her yard had broken, so she sent another of the girls with a paint bucket three doors down to a neigh-bor's to buy water. It cost one gourde, about three cents. The water went into a pot, which was placed on the fire on the stove. Then a few minutes later, Louisilia dumped the beans into the boiling water.

Preparation continued. Family members not involved in the meal—the males and the young—sat and waited patiently in the yard. Two teenage girls peeled leeks. Dieumène washed mangoes. Louisilia, before sitting down to cut fat from the chicken pieces, took a pinch of salt from a cube and sprinkled it into the boiling beans. She sat on a flaking cinder block in the yard. Dieumène sat on a mat in the far corner of the yard, away from the fire and the occasional blowing ash. She sifted through the rice, tossing handfuls into the air and letting it fall onto the bamboo.

Overall, the scene was one of a party. Girls combed and braided each other's hair. Three boys played marbles in the yard. They drew a circle with their fingers in the dirt and tried to dislodge their opponents' marbles by shooting other marbles at them with their thumb. Marbles are some of the only toys I saw in Trou Sable. Most toys were makeshift at best. Across Louisilia's yard, in a puddle of water near the pump, sat an empty plastic quart of motor oil that had been turned into a toy car. I'd seen one made essentially the same way at Rosemène's market stand in 2006. The spout was the hood, to which a string had been attached for a child to pull. Turned on its side, the container had two axles poked through it with buttons affixed to the ends for tires. A passenger slot had been cut out of the other side.

Ketia Brunel, Louisilia's daughter, scooped the clean rice into the pot of beans on the stove. She added more water and spices, including tomato sauce mixed with butter. Louisilia then called Tony and told him to feed the chickens. He walked to corner of the walled-in yard and picked up two chickens tied together at the feet. Tony carried them to the area where Dieumène had sifted the rice. The chickens knew what to do. They were to eat the grains of rice that had been thrown out. They would have to be fattened up before being slaughtered in a week or two for a meal.

Louisilia had placed her cut chicken into a pan on the stove to fry. She added bouillon cubes and then went to work on the thick mixture of rice and beans, stirring it with a large metal spoon. She also prepared thin gravy. When the chicken had fried, she placed it into a serving pan. At that point, she went inside the house and cleared a spot on the floor in the first room near her table. She would serve from there. Using a blue towel as a hot pad, she carried first the dish of chicken pieces and then the gravy into the house and put them on the floor. Then she brought in the rice and beans. Beside her sat a bamboo basket containing the family's plates, bowls, and utensils.

Louisilia scooped the rice and beans into thirteen bowls. She knew who would receive each one and divided the food in accordance to the recipient's size and age. After all the rice had been divvied up, she placed a piece of chicken in each dish and ladled sauce onto each serving. Four plates went up onto the table, where the four males would eat. It was Haitian custom. Tony, the oldest male in the house, was served first.

A serving was taken to the widow who lived next door in the duplex. Then Louisilia called each family member by name and handed them their dinner. Some would eat the rice with their fingers.

Dieumène was second to last. She took her dinner out into the yard and sat near her daughters. Louisilia scraped the main serving bowl clean of rice and beans. Labor completed, she took up her bowl and walked to a chair in the yard to eat.

Edele Henrisma bent at the waist over a charcoal fire in the sheet-metal shack that is her kitchen. A makeshift grill straddled a pile of gray, dusty briquettes; a stainless steel pot held rice. She lifted the lid with her left hand, protected from the heat by a white cloth napkin, and stirred the contents with a metal teaspoon. Beside the rice container was another stainless steel pot with a metal strainer atop it. In the strainer rested a handful of green leafy vegetables. A fistful of warmed black beans filled what was the equivalent of a cereal bowl on the dirt floor.

Rain started to fall hard. A small stream formed in the hard-packed dirt and trailed into the kitchen. A loud crack of thunder accompanied a flash of dull lightning. Three Henrisma children, sitting adjacent to the kitchen on the side porch of the three-room house, jerked their heads skyward, startled.

Edele knelt, scraping a new path in the dirt in an effort to redirect the water back outside of the kitchen. Her solution was effective until the rain came down more heavily. Her husband, Johnny, retrieved a shovel from their bedroom, where he stores his tools. He cleared dirt from beneath the corrugated metal wall, allowing water to run out more easily.

The process of preparing dinner was not without its challenges, even after the greatest obstacle—coming up with the money to buy the food—had been met. Johnny brought out two white paint buckets he had just bought. He placed one beneath a corner where two gutters meet. The overflow fell into the bucket. The family will use the water for washing, possibly for drinking, too. Rainwater, Johnny said, is cleaner and safer to drink than the well water they normally use.

Earlier in the afternoon, Johnny and Edele had sent their son Nelson and another boy, Tigar, Edele's godson who was living with them temporarily, to an in-home shop down the street for a few ounces of cooking oil. The boys had placed a yellow plastic margarine container with a lid into a stainless steel bucket with a handle. Nelson is four years older than Tigar, but Tigar is taller. Nelson was eleven years old. Tigar was seven. Edele said Nelson almost died when he was younger. His parents bought a coffin. The plates of his skull separated. They had to take him to a hospital in Port-au-Prince, where doctors could not tell the family what was wrong, Edele said.

Tigar and Nelson walked to the market, unchaining the crude lock on the sheet-metal gate, turning right down a narrow path toward the main street of the neighborhood. Tigar, dressed in black jeans and a green collared shirt with three buttons, extended his right hand to hold Nelson's left hand. Nelson, dressed in ripped blue jeans and a Tonka T-shirt with the number 01 across the chest, gripped the bucket in his right hand. They proceeded to the market, where a woman used a ladle to dole out a few ounces of cooking oil.

Back at home, daughter Dieuna had awakened from a nap. She has a spot where she sleeps during the day. It is just inside the door of the parlor, on the bare, cool, pink-tinted concrete floor. She sweated in her sleep and left a damp outline of her head and neck—like a penumbra—on the concrete.

The family had not eaten all day. Yet Edele and Johnny invited Augustin and me to stay and share their meal. We said no thank you but were grateful for their kindness.

Once or twice a week, the Henrisma family will go without food for at least a day.

"The children are happy to have dinner," Johnny said. "They were happy when they saw the food. They did not expect that. God sent us food."

The food being prepared for dinner was the only food

in the house. There is no pantry in which canned goods or other nonperishables are stored. The meal would be eaten on the side porch, where the family spends much of its daylight hours. A prayer of thanksgiving would be said before dinner:

Bless us, O Lord,
And these thy gifts
Which we are about to receive
From thy bounty,
Through Christ, our Lord
Amen

In the course of three visits to Haiti, which totaled about five weeks, I shared dozens of meals with my hosts. As impolite as this statement might sound, I have watched them eat.

Every fiber of a small piece of chicken, including cartilage and softer bone, is consumed. Each grain of rice is eaten off the plate. A Haitian is not likely to toss out a bruised spot on a banana. Many times on the street, a Haitian child, occasionally naked, has pulled on my shirt or the hair on my arms. "Blan, give me ten gourdes," the child will say in well-rehearsed English. "I am hungry."

In the two trips I made to Haiti in 2006 and 2008 for this book, the father of one of my three featured families, Johnny Henrisma, twice said while saying goodbye that he regretted he could not entertain me in his home for a meal. Though I am a self-confessed picky eater—no condiments or salad dressing, for starters—I have always tried to be a member of what my mother called the clean-plate club.

Yet, I realized in Haiti, cutting down on food waste means more than just eating what's on your plate. Just before my 2008 trip to Port-au-Prince and Gonaïves, I threw away half a bag of romaine lettuce that I had let go brown in my refrigerator. Same with a container of leftover green beans that was probably still good. Then there was the helping of pork and beans I had let go cold and crusted in the pan on the stove while I watched a baseball game on television with my sixteen-year-old son. And what about those three or four cups of yogurt that had gone uneaten past their expiration date? And the third of a jar of spoiled spaghetti sauce that perpetually exists behind the jugs of milk and orange juice.

Globally, twenty-five thousand people a day die of hunger.[2] The United States throws away ninety-six billion—yes, that's a "b"—pounds of food a year; that's 320 pounds per person. I personally eat out of boredom or in reaction to stress. I am part of the global food crisis. I have to do better.

Chapter 13

June 26–29, 2008

Physical change over time in Gonaïves is subtle, not obvious, unless there is a natural disaster. The city was in its fourth year without a flood by the time I came back in June 2008 to see the three families. The landscape was largely unchanged. A hurricane would hit two months later, causing widespread flooding and more deaths.

The hardness of daily life did show on the sometimes frail bodies and hollowed faces of the Henrisma, Cénécharles, and Louis families. In the streets and homes, there wasn't as much outward optimism expressed as there had been two years earlier. The members of these families were hungry and fighting off the diseases and fatigue—overall lethargy— that accompany such an acute shortage of food.

"Bad to worse" was a common phrase used by people in Gonaïves to describe their lives in 2008.

Still, the Haitians I saw and knew rose from bed every morning before the sun, determined to make the most of the new day, despite the many obstacles in front of them. They clung to the stubborn hope that today would be better than yesterday, and they were willing to do their part to make it happen. They would search for a way to buy or acquire food, perpetually borrowing money to meet even the most basic of human needs. They would try to find work. They would go to school. They would fix up their houses. And at the end of the day, though bone weary, they would have kept their dignity intact and found reasons to believe.

Shelter: Home Improvements

Somewhat to my surprise, two years after I had met them, the three families maintained the same homes. The neighborhood and the people living there, in many ways, were less transient and more stable than I had anticipated. They had held their ground against mounting obstacles brought on by the worsening economy in their homeland, already the most impoverished in the western hemisphere. They had maintained a sense of order, like the American middle class. Moreover, these three Haitian families had each found ways to make improvements on their homes in the two-year span between my visits.

Edele Henrisma had bought a string of white icicle Christmas lights and hung it diagonally from the ceiling of her parlor. Tiny white lights hang from threads of the main electrical cord. The illusion created is that of illuminated icicles, most often hung from the fronts of homes in the United States during the Christmas holiday season. She said she thinks they are pretty, even if the family does not have a constant source of electricity to light them. Edele keeps her family in clean clothes and her house as neat and sanitary as possible. She did sell some of her household items: a wire set of shelves on which she stored dishes and pots, as well as some of the dishes and pots themselves. She sold two of her favorite dresses as well, all in an effort to get money for increasingly expensive food staples, such as rice.

Louisilia had pulled together enough money to buy a kitchen table and four chairs, which have wirelike white backs. The table is rectangular and covered with a tan-and-white-striped tablecloth. She also purchased two shelves of pressed wood, with a finish the color of oak. On it she has piled coffee cups and plates of a solid orange color and a matching set of black and white coffee cups and saucers. A bouquet of yellow artificial flowers rises out of a drinking glass on which there is an image of a cardinal. To make room for the table and shelves, she moved one of the twin beds to her back bedroom, where it is squeezed in with her queen-size bed.

Fritz Cénécharles said in 2006 that, when he had the money, he would build an enclosed kitchen to replace the freestanding one in the yard built of wood and sheet metal. With the help of his friend Johnny Henrisma, Fritz did follow through on that plan. Now, between the enclosed shower and outhouse in a back corner of his property, rose a concrete kitchen with three permanent burners built into a concrete base. Plastic and stainless steel bowls and other pots and pans are stacked on a shelf across from the stove. The roof is sheet metal, like those of the adjacent rooms.

There's a kitchen window that offers a look back toward the main house. The opening is covered with metal rebar, three rods running horizontally across the space, five rods vertically. On the window sill of this dark room, silhouetted against the backdrop of daylight, rest the basic tools used in this kitchen: two boxes of matches, a small oil lamp, a bowl with handles in which there are a few green leaves, and a heavy clay mortar and pestle.

Work: "He Had to Go"

Fritz and Johnny built the kitchen before Fritz went overseas for the third time looking for work. He left in April 2007. It was now June 2008. He had been gone fifteen months and would be gone for another year.

"He is in hiding," said his wife, Rosemène. "He is not legal. Sometimes he gets work. Sometimes he does not."

I sat with Rosemène and Augustin on the porch of the family home in Trou Sable. The midday sun beat down from a cloudless blue sky. Fritz had flown from Port-au-Prince to Curaçao, an island in the southern Caribbean Sea off the coast of Venezuela.

He will send home whatever money he can make from his odd jobs. He works about two or three days out of every month. Not good, his wife said, but better than he could do in Haiti. Fritz has a cell phone. He calls. He talks to Rosemène. He talks with Mackenson, his oldest child.

"God shows me what to do," Rosemène said of her life without her husband. "Life is expensive here. Education is expensive here. He had to go."

The family does not appear to be as well emotionally, or as healthy or stable, as it was two years earlier. Fritz is gone. Food shortages and inflation have made it more expensive to live day to day. Business is suffering at Rosemène's home goods and clothing booth in the Gonaïves market. The city cleared many vendors off Liberty Street and moved them inside a large market building. The location is not as good, she said. People are doing without buying clothing and are stretching household items in order to spend a higher percentage of the little they have on food.

Each member of the Cénécharles family has lost weight. Their three youngest children, including Wisly, are more lethargic and less energetic. Wisly sleeps with his mother in his parents' bed. "To protect her," he said. He does not understand why his father had to leave.

Fritz had again ridden a rickety bus south from Gonaïves to Port-au-Prince and the country's international airport. The former U.S. school buses are repainted bright blue and red and decorated in white lettering to offer ironic and sometimes cruel phrases of optimism: "Patience is a virtue." "Jesus is with you."

Fritz lives in Curaçao with friends from Haiti who are there legally. "They help him a lot," Rosemène said. The friends feed him. They give him free rent.

"It is difficult," Rosemène said of life without Fritz. "When the father is absent, the whole family is affected. The family thinks about him a lot."

Fritz is not the only man from the community out of the country in search of work. Oril Louis, the widower brother of Louisilia Louis, had returned to the Dominican Republic, which shares the island of Hispaniola with Haiti. He, too, is a mason.

As of June 2008, he has been gone two months. Louisilia has not heard from him. She cares for his daughter, Micheline, born in 2004. "She is not healthy," Louisilia said of the girl. "I cannot afford to take her to the hospital." Her other children and those of her widowed sister also are ill.

"The children are not fed well, so they are sick," said Louisilia, who wants to work and earn money to care for her family. "I have one thing in my mind now: I would like to set up a business, like Mackenson's mother."

In the meantime, in a community and nation ravaged by unemployment, hunger, and illness, Louisilia turns constantly to prayer. "The children are in God's hands," she said. "I believe in God. I believe God hears my prayers." Is she angry with God? After all, she cannot find work and is unable to feed her children for days at a time. "No, no, I am not angry," she said. "You are not to get angry with God. You are to pray to God."

Johnny Henrisma prays, too. And on a Friday morning during my visit he is hard at work repairing a wall he built several years earlier. The home he is working on is owned by a fellow parishioner from Holy Family Catholic Church. "I have a whole day of work," he said.

There are specks of gray mortar on the black skin of his arms, face, and neck. He wears a white hard hat. He wields a trowel, picking up the cement mix and slapping it onto the exterior wall.

"The salt destroys the walls," he said in reference to the floods caused in 2004 by rains from the tropical storm. The client, in this case, a single woman who sews for a living, bought the necessary materials. Johnny told her what to buy. The woman, Gertrude Novembre, age forty-two years in 2008, is the godmother of Johnny's son, Dieunel, who mixes the cement for his father in the yard. Dieunel turns over the sand, water, and cement mix with a shovel, then slices the mushy pile into sections with the shovel before repeating the process.

How much is the homeowner paying Johnny per hour? Is there a set price for his labor and time? "No. I will get something," Johnny said. "She is a member of the church. She will give me what she has. She is a very good person. She is very helpful to the people here. She shares what she has. I just cannot charge her."

Even in a neighborhood where chaos appears to reign, there is order. There is a community of people, a network of neighbors who share their time and talents with each other. As Johnny works on the wall, Gertrude sits on her front porch, fixing holes in clothing on her manual sewing machine. She powers it with a foot pedal. She is divorced with one child, a daughter. She lives with her daughter and three sisters.

"If I could afford it, I would paint the walls," she said. "It helps to keep them strong. After seven years, I decided to repair the walls. Johnny built the walls [in August 2001]. I know Johnny. I know his family. I trust him. He is a good mason. I know he does good work. We share. If the mason is your friend, he will do the work for you."

Johnny smiles. He is happy to be working, even though the pay might not be equal to his ten-hour labor. At the end of the day, Johnny will walk home and wear a smile on his face. Working is better than not, even if he receives little or no immediate pay.

Edele waits at home for her husband. There is a little food, some okra and rice. The family will have a meal with very small portions but will eat nonetheless. The children will go to bed at sunset. Johnny and Edele will go to their room.

"I rub his back and give him a massage at night when he has worked," Edele said. "I rub his arms and shoulders. He is very tired and sore. I count on him. He counts on me. He says sweet things to me."

Johnny and other Haitians need comfort where they can find it. The average life span in Haiti barely reaches into the fifties. Hard lives—marked by shortages of food, clean water, and medical care—physically age the body prematurely. Along with the accelerated aging process comes emotional maturity.

The oldest children in each of these families, all sons, possess hard-won wisdom beyond their years. Mackenson Cénécharles turned twenty-one in 2008, and Dieunel Henrisma and Tony Cémouin turned eighteen. They all talk of their faith in God and hope in the future, despite the crippling poverty and dim prospects in their homeland. It's as though they are keenly aware of the reality of their lives but cannot allow themselves to fully comprehend or verbalize it. They must remain optimistic to get from day to day. There is sadness edged into their words and body language. Their bodies slump, as if deflated, when asked about what tomorrow holds for them.

With his father, Fritz, overseas, Mackenson has been thrust into a position of responsibility. Mackenson is heading into his last year of high school and dreams, like his mother did as a girl, of being a civil engineer. He has finished trade school, where he studied photography, and is now learning how to play guitar. He is the man of the house. That role is primary in Mackenson's life. "I feel that the father is the head of the family," he said. "When he is not in the house, something is missing. We feel sad."

Like the other members of his family, Mackenson has lost a great deal of weight in two years because of the shortage of food. The watch Mackenson wears on his left wrist hangs loose. "I have to help my mom," Mackenson said. "We have to sit and find a solution if there is a problem. We have to decide together."

Dieunel is heading into the tenth grade. He still hopes to be a doctor. He studies as a hobby because there is little else to do. When his father, Johnny, does find work, Dieunel goes with him and makes the concrete mix. "As long as there is life, there is hope," Dieunel said. "I hope everything will change."

Two of his siblings died as babies.

"The economic situation has affected my family mentally and physically," Dieunel said. "But I have to believe that as long as we are with God things are going to change."

Tony talks openly of his faith that God will provide. "Even when we don't eat," he said, "God keeps us strong."

He is headed into the sixth grade. He started school late. He plans to finish his studies in medicine. Away from school, he helps his mother, Louisilia, with the house. He cooks when they have food. He cleans their two-room home. "I take responsibility for the house when she is gone," he said.

Tony likes to watch his friends play marbles. In 2006 when we spoke, he talked at length of being afraid to go outside because of gangs and gunshots. He would hide under his bed. In one respect, despite the food crisis, life is better. "There is peace now. There is no more violence," he said.

It could come back. Gangs come and go. So does the gunfire. The constants in his life, he said, are faith and hope that he will have a chance at a better life than his mother. To think otherwise would be to lose. "I have to be optimistic," he said. "I cannot give up."

Clothing: One Pair of Pants

On Friday, a woman came by the shop owned and run by Rosemène Cénécharles. The woman wanted a pair of black jeans. Rosemène did not have her size in stock but suggested she see if another size would fit. The customer held up the pants to the front of her body. They would not fit.

Rosemène said little about the near miss on the transaction, other than to repeat that business was bad because people now had to spend more money on food, which had tripled in price. Her son Wisly was at work with her. Near lunchtime, she handed him a few gourdes to get a treat. Nine-year-old Wisly walked to a nearby food stand and bought a plastic tube of flavored ice—lime green. He returned to his mother's booth and sat on a stack of packaged bed sheets and ate the ice. He pushed it up from the bottom with his index finger and thumb.

On Saturday, Rosemène left Wisly in the care of his older brother and sisters and took a bus to Port-au-Prince in order to restock her shop. The trip, on former U.S. school buses that are so overcrowded that people ride on top of the roof, is not an easy one. The national highway that connects Gonaïves with Port-au-Prince is, at best, a two-lane blacktop. But most of the roadway was washed out by Hurricane Jeanne in 2004. (Subsequent floods later in 2008 would do further damage.) At points, the roadway is little more than compacted soil. It is deeply rutted. Vehicles travel all over the road, both on the left and right sides, looking for the smoothest surface. The round trip, though a total of just 120 miles, takes six hours.

On Sunday morning, Rosemène and Wisly walked from their home to Holy Family Catholic Church for six-thirty Mass. It was Father's Day. Wisly said that he missed his dad. Rosemène carried a thin, black plastic bag with her into church. In it were a handful of items she had bought the day before in Port-au-Prince, including black jeans in the size of the woman who had been by the shop Friday.

After Mass, Rosemène and Wisly would walk to the market. On the way to the market, Rosemène planned to make a house call. She would stop at the woman's home with the right size of black jeans and ask if she still wanted to buy them.

Widow Louisilia Louis manages to provide another meal—chicken and rice with a handful of vegetables—to her family, June 2008.

A rare toy for a Haitian child, a pull toy cut from a motor oil container, in the Louis yard, June 2008.

Louisilia Louis and her extended family, thirteen in all, live in a two-room house, May 2006.

Micheline Louis, born to her Haitian father, Oril Louis, in the Dominican Republic, is now motherless, June 2008.

Louisilia Louis prepares her family's meals on a charcoal stove, June 2008.

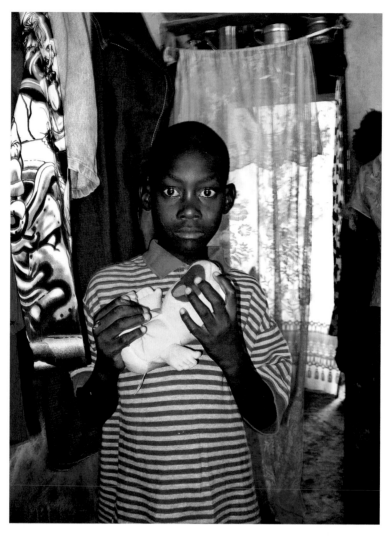

Poor Haitian families often have a stuffed animal—here a frog—as a pet, or *nou nous*, May 2006.

Haitian women favor artificial flowers to inject color into an otherwise drab, gray environment, May 2006.

The young women in the Louis household are among the many Haitians who buy and wear used American clothing, June 2008. The United States discards an estimated 2.5 billion pounds of textiles a year, as much as 80 percent of it finding its way to third-world markets such as Haiti.

Family photos and a calendar adorn a wall in the Louis home, May 2006.

Oril Louis leaves his young daughter with his widowed sisters in Gonaïves and travels to the neighboring Dominican Republic to find work as a mason, May 2006.

Life goes on in Port-au-Prince following the earthquake. A painter sells his wares in the shell of his destroyed home, March 2010.

Tens of thousands of concrete homes hang precariously on steep hillsides in and around Port-au-Prince, making them susceptible to earthquake damage, March 2010.

A displaced family takes refuge in a "tent city" near the international airport in Port-au-Prince, March 2010.

A boy tucks a donated spray bottle of Lysol cleaner in his shirt in the courtyard of a damaged school in Calebasse, about fifteen miles southeast of downtown Port-au-Prince, March 2010.

Synthia Jovin, thirteen, peeks from behind the gate of a school in the
Port-au-Prince neighborhood of Fontamara, March 2010.

Like many young Haitians, Synthia Jovin shows wisdom beyond her years, March 2010.

Foreign nonprofit groups tried to help get schools back in session within weeks of the January 12 earthquake. Here, students attend class in the Fontamara neighborhood of Port-au-Prince, March 2010.

Even two months following the high-magnitude earthquake, many buildings remain untouched piles of rubble in Port-au-Prince, entombing the decaying bodies of victims, March 2010.

Chapter 14

A Promise in Haiti

The end of my second trip to Haiti created in me a sense of relief. My endurance for the shorter 2008 visit was not nearly as strong as it had been in 2006, when I stayed for nearly three weeks. This time, I looked forward to going home to Cincinnati after six days and five nights.

My departure nonetheless brought sadness. Sunday, June 29, 2008, was my last day in Gonaïves. I would ride that afternoon to Port-au-Prince and fly to Miami the next day. I remember thinking how unlikely it would be that I would come back. I wouldn't need to, I said to myself. I had gathered all of the information and material I would need to finish my book.

I was up Sunday morning at five thirty to make it to six-thirty Mass at Holy Family Church. I rode from the Hands Together compound on the edge of town, where had I stayed, into the city. Father Gérard Dormévil, the Holy Family pastor and my host, drove a light construction truck. Augustin sat in the middle of the bench seat. I squeezed in, next to the passenger door.

Father Gérard stopped to pick up a woman and her young son, probably seven or eight years old, on the way to Mass. Smiling, they waited on a corner, pinned against an

161

unpainted cinder-block wall whenever a vehicle passed by. The woman wore a white skirt with a floral pattern of red, green and yellow. Her son had on khaki dress pants and a white golf shirt with a collar. Before I realized what was happening, they climbed into the bed of the truck, where they would have to hold tightly to a railing against the wind and jostling from the deeply rutted roads. (On the return trip, I made sure Augustin and I stood in the back and that they rode in the cab.)

It was Father's Day in Haiti, two weeks later than I had celebrated with my three children in the United States. At Mass, the Haitian fathers in the congregation all dressed in suits and ties. Father Gérard called them "dapper" during his homily. Everyone else in the church laughed politely. He encouraged the men to take from the examples of Saints Paul and Peter in their roles as fathers, husbands, and leaders in the community.

Johnny Henrisma wore a black suit, red tie, and white shirt. The jacket was baggy on his thinning body; he had lost weight—ten pounds at least off his five-foot, eight-inch frame—in the two years since I had met him. He weighed 140 pounds tops, probably less. His high cheekbones appeared to protrude more; the hollows of his lower face cut deeper. The collar of his dress shirt fit loosely around his neck. It bunched because of the tight knot in his tie. I watched him throughout the service, clutching his hymnal and singing each song fervently, as though the intensity of his prayer would increase its chance of being heard.

Louisilia Louis sat in the pew in front of me and to my left. She wore a blue-jean skirt and white T-shirt. I sat beside Augustin, who was thirty-eight and had now traveled twice with me from his home in Port-au-Prince.

At the sign of peace, the point in the Mass when people greet each other in the pews, Louisilia went out of her way to get to me. She gripped my right hand with both of hers. She patted the back of my hand with her left palm. After Mass, we said goodbye. I held my arms out toward her and open upward. Louisilia grasped my forearms from the top and squeezed. We both fought back tears. Neither she nor I said, "See you again." It was a simple "Orevwa" (goodbye).

Then I talked with Johnny, who stood in the school yard with the other fathers from the choir. He told me again that he was sorry he did not have enough money to entertain me in his home with a meal. Through Augustin, I told Johnny to please not feel badly. His sentiment was more than enough. I said I understood. He shook my hand and placed his left hand on my right shoulder.

Then I visited briefly with Rosemène Cénécharles and her son Wisly. As she had done in 2006 when she said goodbye, Rosemène clasped her hands behind her and leaned into me to kiss each of my cheeks. Wisly shook my hand. In 2006, he had told me he wanted to live with me in the United States. He had hugged me goodbye then. He was less affectionate in 2008. Daily life in Haiti had taken a toll on Wisly. He had been forced to grow up quickly in the absence of his father and faced with the harsh realities of life. There was less time for playing and more responsibility to contribute to the household.

As they walked down the street, a nine-year-old boy beside the mother he adored, my mind took me back thirty-five years to a similar scene in Dixon, Illinois. I saw myself walking home from Mass with my mother, Elizabeth Curnutte. I wanted so badly to please her and my father at every turn. I often carried my little brother, Spence, on my shoulders as we walked. The hymn "Whatsoever You Do" came to mind. It was often played at Masses of my boyhood at St. Patrick Church:

Whatsoever you do to the least of my people
That you do unto me

Nothing in my faith has ever made as much sense to me as the idea that you have to earn salvation by your works in this life. We are to believe that Jesus is in every person, especially those people the world would define as disposable. Why would they teach me that song as a child if it weren't true? Was Thomas Merton correct? Does the earthly poverty of others exist, in part, to reveal to us the poverty of our own souls? Do natural disasters—hurricanes, floods, earthquakes, and drought, piled atop poverty—occur simply as random acts or as tests and opportunities presented by God to see how we, the fortunate, respond?

I thought of the mission appeal I was scheduled to make on behalf of the Diocese of Gonaïves in a parish in Lorain, Ohio, three weeks later. In all the years that I'd been asking for money for development work in Haiti, one passage from the Bible best explained the balance to strike in what to keep and what to give to the poor. (I'm no scholar, believe me; I check out the assigned weekend readings and gospel online.) The passage is from 2 Corinthians: "Not that others should have relief while you are burdened; but that as a matter of equality your abundance at this present time should supply their needs."

As I stood on the dirt street in front of Holy Family's gate in Trou Sable, even more disparate yet related thoughts collided; more questions poured in, far many more questions than answers. What have I done with my good fortune of being born to my parents and in the United States? Why do I still complain about parts of my life? Why am I anxious? I thought about the people I'd come to know and like in Gonaïves. Why did they have so little when I and others had so much? What could or would I do about it? Why wouldn't I do more? How will God judge me for what I have not done with the many gifts given to me? What is expected of me, having been given the opportunity to know these Haitian people and experience, even in relative safety, their daily lives?

In *Let Us Now Praise Famous Men*, James Agee fervently hoped that the poverty he witnessed in Hale County, Alabama, would cease: "Let us know, let us know there is a cure to it, there is to be an end to it" (p. 439). Here on the street in Gonaïves, I tried to stop thinking. I tried to stop being emotional. I wanted to capture the scene. Two chickens pecked in a muddy puddle. The mixture of burning charcoal and animal waste was especially pungent. The grit from the street blew into my face, the oily residue of others' hands collected between my fingers. A baby cried from an open-air house. Beads of sweat rolled down the middle of my back beneath the T-shirt I wore under my dress shirt. The sky was light blue, almost pale. I scribbled key words in my notebook—chickens, stench, dirt, sweat, sky. At the same time, I wanted to pray. I was overwhelmed intellectually and emotionally. Would I ever see these people again?

I started to recite in my mind the Our Father. I stopped at the line "Thy will be done." I repeated it. It made more sense than ever. Later I would learn to repeat the line ten times, one hundred, if needed. Your will, God, not mine; I would interpret what that phrase meant in other words to try to make it better stick.

You're in charge, God, not me.

You know all, I know little.

I trust you.

I need to do better.

Give me the strength to follow your lead.

The writing process yielded some answers but even more questions. If I had the solution to the poverty in Haiti, I'd have won a Nobel Prize by now. Is there a solution? Surrender to God's will: easy to profess, more difficult to live.

My journey into the heart of Haiti had turned into a journey into my own heart. I would no longer mindlessly consider food, shelter, and easy access to clean water as common comforts I'm entitled to. I am now especially grateful for safe tap water when I brush my teeth. I can't help but view multi-course, sixty-dollar meals in restaurants and two-thousand-square-foot houses as wildly excessive. How much do I really need? Is my standard of living robbing millions of people around the world of basic needs?

I was growing more Christian and less Catholic—or ecumenical, not even Christian—less attracted to ritual and tradition and ceremony and more attuned to the responsibility we have to the world's neediest people. I had experienced success at work; I had gotten good at my job. Elsewhere in my life—spiritually, as a father, as a man—I learned how far I had fallen behind. I struggle mightily with dislike and distrust for my ex-wife, allowing them sometimes to partially conceal the love I have for my children. Divorced, I sense an excommunication of sorts from the Catholic Church. I am really no longer a member of that club. Had I been too plugged in to the earthly church, surrounded by too many people who looked, talked, and acted just like me, comfortable, a face in the crowd, anonymous, otherwise disconnected from my higher power, racing through life so as to blur its details, reluctant to stand alone and face my mortality and many shortcomings?

Somewhere in the fifth or sixth draft of this chapter, it occurred to me that maybe God gave me the passion for Haiti and opportunity to travel there to help me finally understand a fact that I could recite intellectually. It's not all in this world. God had broken me down, maybe to help me better empathize with the people I'd meet and write about in Haiti. Soon after I returned home from Haiti in the summer of 2008, that internal brokenness began to express itself through anxiety that either fluttered across the top of my chest cavity or weighed heavily like a metal rod, resting under my sternum. Pain was no longer a concept. It was a reality in middle age, a suffocating fear of being alone and wondering what the remaining years of life will bring.

I prayed: God, help me to trust you more.

On the street in Trou Sable, I had fixed my gaze on Rosemène and Wisly. He held tightly to his mother's right hand as they walked down the dirt street. The little boy both needed her and wanted to be needed. He needed her protection and wanted to protect her. They would turn the corner to their left and disappear in a few seconds—into the sea of humanity in the market where two days earlier I had watched Louisilia Louis buy rice and chicken. I thought of Rosemène's struggle to hold her family together in her husband's absence. Fritz Cénécharles was essentially island hopping in the Caribbean in his ongoing effort to find work. I thought of the economic injustice that forced him from the wife and children he loves. Their family was the healthiest of any I'd seen in Haiti, the most easy to relate with. It was a progressive family. Fritz had stayed home, watched the children, and run the household. Rosemène was the breadwinner. They had adapted to conditions. Still, they were not immune to the devastating poverty and worsening food crisis.

I thought of Fritz, whom I like and respect. I had been

disappointed when I learned upon my arrival in Gonaïves a few days earlier that he had gone overseas again. Selfishly, I wanted to speak with him. I recalled one of our conversations toward the end of my visit in 2006.

Through Augustin, I had lamented that I was not a doctor, nurse, lawyer, nutritionist, engineer, politician, or even a priest—someone, anyone, who could do more to help improve living conditions for Fritz's family and those around him. Fritz interrupted me and spoke directly and precisely to Augustin in Creole; Fritz, I sensed, wanted to make sure I understood what he was about to tell me. Fritz said I was not intended to be any of those professions. I was supposed to be a writer, and I was supposed to come to Haiti to write about his and the other two families.

"Jesus brought you here," he said several times.

Fritz's words to me were important. They became the spine to which I connected every detail of this story. Still, though humbled by Fritz's idea of my purpose, I suspected that Jesus had more important things to be concerned about than me.

I remember saying goodbye to Fritz in his front yard in May 2006. We shook hands after we spoke and looked each other in the eye. He had done his part. He opened his family's life to me. He allowed me to ask intensely personal questions. He let me poke around his home without interference. It was my turn to honor my end of the deal. I would write about them.

More than embracing any sweeping program or suggesting that the United States and other countries pour even more foreign aid into Haiti—or committing political blasphemy as an American and suggesting that Haiti would benefit from a socialist government, to break up the wealth of an oppressive few for the good of the oppressed many—I came to understand that maybe the most important statement I could make was to persevere and write about these three Haitian families and their community. If the world would listen just once in my lifetime to one thing I had to say, what would it be? See these families. Let them in.

My promise to Fritz provided motivation when motivation seriously lagged. What's more, if I truly believed that he and I are equals, I had to keep the promise.

Afterword

Under the Mango Tree

For just a moment, the driver lost control of the pickup. It jerked sharply to the right before he could guide it safely to the shoulder. The front axle had fallen off the inside of the right wheel, and the head of the heavy bar dragged a narrow trench in the asphalt, showing the point of separation and the path to the edge of the road. I sat with three others in the back of the tap-tap on the road to Gonaïves on the morning of Sunday, February 28, 2010. The breakdown happened in St. Marc, about half an hour north of our overnight stay in Montrouis.

It was our sixth day in Haiti. My employer, the *Cincinnati Enquirer*, had sent me there with staff photographer Carrie Cochran. Our assignment was to report on the efforts of local relief groups to provide food, medicine, medical care, and other post-earthquake relief supplies. The immediate emergency stage had passed in Haiti by the time we had arrived; the lives that could be saved had been saved, though thousands more were expected to be lost in dangerous squatter camps or from disease. Tens of thousands more people were feared dead already, entombed in mounds of concrete and cinder-block rubble that had yet to be searched.

Augustin and Tony Mitchell, a disaster relief volunteer from Lebanon, Ohio, rode with Carrie and me in the back of the tap-tap. We had hired the driver, Mackenson, for one hundred U.S. dollars plus the cost of a tank of gas. The sun had risen in a cloudless sky, and the air had yet to be fogged with smoke from charcoal fires. Many people walked beside the road on their way to church. Men wore dark suits, white shirts, and ties. Women wore dresses. Girls in floral skirts and blouses and polished black leather shoes tiptoed around puddles and stepped lightly in the mud, holding hands for safety. A few vendors already were out, selling fruit, sixteen-ounce bottles of Coke and Sprite, chewing gum, bread, and clothing.

Our plan for the day was ambitious. Getting from point A to point B is hard enough in Haiti, even when the nation is not reeling from a natural disaster. Trips always take longer than anticipated. Even generous time estimates are too narrow. There are always complications, such as a broken axle. I knew we were trying to do too much.

Our first stop would be Hôpital Albert Schweitzer near the rural north-central town of Deschapelles, the heart of the agricultural Artibonite Valley. We had an appointment to speak with Cincinnati native Dawn Johnson, hospital coordinator of potable water and sanitation, as well as director Ian Rawson, son of cofounder Gwen Mellon. The hospital serves 300,000 people from a 615-square-mile area in Haiti's central swath. Yet on the night of the earthquake and in the following days, hundreds more found their way there from Port-au-Prince. More than eight hundred injured people, strapped to doors that served as makeshift stretchers, were brought by friends and family members in the backs of tap-taps. The hospital staff of sixteen doctors and fifty nurses, all Haitians, cared for everyone who needed care.

Our second stop that Sunday would be Gonaïves. I had hoped to visit for a couple of hours with the Cénécharles,

172

Henrisma, and Louis families. I wanted to see them badly, more as friends than as the main characters of this book. I also wanted an update on their conditions and to see how they'd been affected by the earthquake, though their city had not sustained direct physical damage.

Our final destination would be back in Montrouis, at the Ebenezer Orphanage, which we had already visited twice. A minister and his wife, who have four children of their own, had taken in twenty-three orphans. As many as sixteen children sleep on mats in a single room of the house. A Cincinnati-based organization, A Child's Hope International, had started a relationship with the orphanage to regularly provide high-protein, prepackaged meals. Food, scarce to begin with, had almost doubled in price since the earthquake. A can of rice that sold for roughly $2.50 U.S. now cost $4. The Ebenezer orphans were sometimes limited to one meal a day or forced to go a day without eating.

One must start small to begin to understand an event as big as Haiti's earthquake. Daily living conditions and the environment are overwhelming, intellectually and emotionally, even in the best of times. A nine-year-old orphan at Ebenezer named Pierre Rooney helped me to see the human aftershock of the quake. "I feel very weak. It hurts to be hungry. I have a bellyache. My head always hurts," he said when I asked him to describe his hunger. I watched Pierre and other children eat lunch on Thursday, February 25. None of the orphans ate quickly. Pierre was especially meticulous. He put only a small bite of rice on his spoon at one time, not even filling it halfway. He moved it slowly toward his face, to ensure he would not drop one grain, and he cleaned the spoon by pulling it back through his clenched lips. Pierre laid his spoon in his metal bowl, rested his forearms on the table, and started to chew. He wanted to concentrate on his meal, making sure to fully acknowledge every bite to create the sensation that his stomach was as full as possible.

I asked him how he had learned to eat so purposefully and why he consumed his food so slowly. "My father," Pierre said. "I don't know when I will get more food." His father could not care for him. Pierre's mother had died. An aunt sent him to the orphanage.

During the meal, I slipped away from the room at the back of the church where the children were eating. Tree limbs and coconut leaves formed the building's walls. A patchwork of blue tarps and other pieces of miscellaneous plastic made up the roof. The church floor was white rock and hard-packed native soil. You feel like a voyeur watching hungry and dying children eat. A reporter's guard fails; emotion happens.

Pierre had taken an instant liking to me just minutes into our first visit to Ebenezer. He grabbed me, claiming me as his *blan*. It was lunchtime. Four bags of food from A Child's Hope International had been portioned to feed the children. I excused myself and walked into the church, where I sat and spread out my arms across the back of a bench. I wanted to just hear the sounds of the orphanage while escaping its sights. Without my knowledge, Pierre had glided into the church, and he was now tucking himself into my left side. He looked up into my face with exhausted dark eyes that were sunken deep into his skull. Inside, my heart pounded with compassion. I could not let out the tears I felt rising. Pierre sighed. My instinct was to pull away; scabies, head lice, and intestinal worms are rampant. That would have been cruel. I sat quietly, my stillness giving Pierre nonverbal permission to drop his head and chest into my thigh. He slung his right arm across my other leg. He was just about asleep when other children burst into the church to find me. They wanted us to join the soccer game starting outside on the rocky soil. The children had no shoes.

I experienced a handful of these types of quiet moments during my ten days back in Haiti, life intersections never to be repeated with people, primarily children, I'd never see again. Sunday night, our last night in Montrouis, Pierre held my hand as we walked up to the orphanage. He turned toward me and hugged my waist, pressing the right side of his head into my stomach, before letting go and walking into the dark building to find his place to sleep.

The next morning, Monday, March 1, we moved our base to Port-au-Prince, where we rented tents to sleep on the soccer field of another church compound, that of the Florida-based World Harvest Mission. Its property stood near Port-au-Prince's international airport, in a neighborhood called Cazeau. A giant mango tree, landscaped with stones and benches to form a large square in its ample shade, greeted visitors inside the World Harvest gate. The grounds contained an orphanage, fish hatchery, and vegetable garden that children tended. Its drinking-water supply was treated with chlorine. Mission organizers had turned their church into a makeshift hospital to treat earthquake victims, mainly children, who needed physical therapy to adjust to life with broken or amputated limbs.

Shakira Thomas, age three years, had lost her left foot. Falling cinder blocks crushed it. I met Shakira, her mother, and her one-year-old brother under the mango tree, where nurses and physical therapists carried children each afternoon on their little mesh cots. In the span of three days, I watched Shakira move from struggling with a walker to mastering crutches.

Another girl, Louise, age twelve, sat on her cot in the hospital. Both of her femurs, broken in the earthquake, were set from the outside with boards and screws and wrapped in gauze. We, too, had met under the mango tree. We communicated nonverbally. I speak very little Creole, despite my ongoing efforts. Louise wanted to see the photos on the identification badges hanging from around my neck on a lanyard. I read her name and age off her yellow hospital bracelet. The smile never left her face, even during painful physical therapy sessions. Unlike some of the other patients, Louise did not have a parent with her. She likely had been orphaned. Later, in the church building after dinner, she motioned for me again. I sat on the concrete floor beside her, and Louise wrapped her gaunt arm around my back. She remembered my name. "Bonswa, Mark." Contemporary gospel music rang through the large room. A few of the other children, even one using a wheelchair, danced with nurses. Louise wanted to dance. So she grabbed my hands. We swung our arms to the beat. We giggled at each other.

In the immediate aftermath of the earthquake, I had thought that no nation was as ill-prepared to handle such a disaster. I learned during my visit after the earthquake that no people were more resilient.

During our final four days in Haiti, March 1–4, we traveled throughout Port-au-Prince and the surrounding area. We went to Petionville, a hillside suburb and home of the Hotel Montana, a four-star lodging with views of the airport and harbor that was a favorite of American and European visitors. The U.S. Mortuary Service was there on the morning we drove to the hotel gate, searching for and removing the bodies of American guests who had died there in the earthquake.

"Orders," said the U.S. Army soldier standing guard. "I can't let anyone in."

Most of the three hundred guests were not in the five-story, 145-room hotel when it collapsed. Still, dozens of people, including U.S. aid workers and college students from Florida, were trapped there and died, according to *USA Today*.[1]

Not far from the hotel, that stubborn and proud agency possessed by many Haitians—the desire to make something out of nothing—was again on display. Many houses on the main road in Petionville had been damaged or destroyed. The back of one house looked out over a deep valley that was now littered with damaged shanties. What caught my eye and caused me to ask our driver to stop was the display of paintings and other artwork in the ruins of the home—as if the artist knew passersby would slow for the breathtaking view. The artist had arranged paintings, including one in a frame and the others stretched on wood backing, along the front of the property and on what used to be the porch.

Yet the countless sites of earthquake damage and buildings reduced to piles of rubble were emotionally and intellectually numbing. I tried to photograph some of them from the bed of our pickup as our driver attempted to move aggressively through heavy traffic. Internally, I attempted to suspend thought, not wanting to imagine how many bodies had already been pulled from the wreckage or, worse, how many bodies were still buried.

We drove to the mountaintop village of Calebasse, about fifteen miles southeast of downtown Port-au-Prince. To get there, you go one mile past where the pavement and guardrails end. The village school had been seriously damaged and was unusable until costly repairs could be made, and its meal program for students was suspended indefinitely. A boy stood in the middle of the playground of the school, rubble piled beneath a swing set to his left, one balcony railing on the ground behind him, another section having falling when the wall beneath it gave way in the earthquake. He had tucked a bottle of Lysol cleaner, a donation, into his T-shirt. Why Lysol, I thought, not food or water? The area's only clinic had been partially destroyed, too, and only two rooms could be occupied safely.

Houses sat on higher ground behind the school. I walked off by myself from the school yard down a trail toward the houses. An elderly woman approached me and took me by the hand, motioning with her other hand for me to follow. I learned that eleven members of Arismé Remy's extended family—six children and five adults—now lived in a tent fashioned from bedsheets. Five twin beds and a queen-size mattress ringed the space. The floor was dirt. The family survived day to day, but food was almost nonexistent, said Remy, age seventy. Her twin granddaughters, Teschna and Fadjouly Remy, age three years, had attended the school. The elderly woman showed me her house, the roof partially collapsed and walls split, the cracked cistern. Normally, the people of Calebasse raise much of their own food and know how to ration water to irrigate during the dry season. Now, however, they were without the means to do so. They needed seeds to plant carrots, cabbage, and other vegetables that can grow in the rocky soil, and many families needed their homes and water cisterns repaired. Life is difficult enough in Calebasse. The earthquake frustrated the proud people who wanted to end a cycle of dependence.

The next two days we traveled throughout Port-au-Prince with Jean-Robert Cadet, a former Haitian child slave and founder in 2007 of the Restavek Foundation, from which he would later in 2010 split to form yet another foundation, called the Jean R. Cadet Restavek Organization. I had met him in 1998, when I wrote in the *Cincinnati Enquirer* about him and his book, *Restavec: From Haitian Slave to Middle-*

Class American (1998). He had met his American wife in Florida and moved with her to her native Greater Cincinnati. Cadet had taught French in a suburban Cincinnati high school before starting the first foundation, the goal of which was to end child servitude in Haiti. An estimated 300,000 children, primarily girls, ages five through fifteen, are kept as domestic slaves. Normally, restavek children do not attend school. Working with families, Cadet convinced owners of 455 restaveks to enroll them in thirty-three different schools. His foundation paid for the children's uniforms and tuition and used these relationships as footholds into whole communities.

"School gives children a piece of normal childhood," Cadet told me during our visit as we walked a street in Carrefour. "If you have broken children, they become broken adults who cannot value any life."

Those schools were the channels through which the foundation's post-earthquake emergency aid programs flowed, including the distribution of fifty thousand dollars worth of food, repair to dozens of damaged schools—hundreds were leveled—and payment of teacher and administration salaries. We visited another school in the Port-au-Prince neighborhood of Fontamara on a steamy March morning. Cadet noted that a restavek boy was not at school, so he walked to his house and returned thirty minutes later with Thomas Feanelom, age eleven, an enslaved child whose mother had died and whose father gave him to another family. If not for Cadet, the boy said, he would not be in school. Thomas, who spoke Creole in a whisper and only to Cadet, said the *loup-garou*— a flying demon or werewolf from French literature—had caused the earthquake. He feared the monster would return and cause another one. The boy had not eaten yet today. Asked what he would like to have, Thomas told Cadet, "Anything you would give me." He received a bowl of rice and beans for lunch at school.

At that school, a young girl asked me to take her picture. Her name was Synthia Jovin; she was thirteen years old and had lived with an aunt since she was three. At first, she darted out from behind an iron gate, only to duck back behind the wall. Finally, she stood still and stared into my camera, her right hand gripping a weathered door frame.

On our last morning in Port-au-Prince, I walked again with Carrie and Augustin around the airport, visiting squatter camps and talking with displaced people. Guilène Mandeus, age thirty, is the married mother of four—the youngest a six-month-old son named Levensky Aleus—whose home in the Croix-des-Missions neighborhood had been destroyed in the earthquake. Her husband was out looking for food and work when we happened upon her. The family home now was a six-by-eight-foot shack fashioned from tree limbs, with sheets and pieces of plastic for its walls and roof. The floor was white rock. A thunderstorm had hit the area the night before, a harbinger of the rainy season. Contaminated water flooded the shanty.

"My house leaks," she said. "I had to stand up last night and hold my baby. He would have drowned." She wore a red sleeveless top and sat in the middle of the tent, holding her baby on her lap.

Nearby, I asked for and received permission to photograph two women sitting in the shade of a red tarp suspended from tree limbs. They sat on what appeared to be two kitchen chairs and used cinder blocks for a table. Outside, on a dirt road, boys played soccer. I walked in their direction. One boy kicked the ball to me. I kicked it to another boy, and he kicked it to Augustin. The soccer pass symbolized something larger. I had become part of the story; so had Augustin.

We had hired Augustin to work for the *Enquirer* on our trip. He met us at the airport and gave me a strong hug. He befriended Carrie and hauled her video camera. "This is mine," he said, smiling. When the U.N. media office refused to give him a credential because he was not on staff, "just" our hired interpreter, I asked him if he wanted the *Enquirer* baseball cap I had brought with me. He wore it. "Part of the team," he said. Augustin made new contacts with leaders of the Cincinnati-area nonprofits, who hired him as an interpreter when they returned.

Yet all was not well, and the human toll of the earthquake and the difficulty of life in Haiti showed on Augustin during our time with him. Just thirty-nine years old, Augustin suffered stress-related seizures in his sleep on two consecutive nights, falling out of bed the second time and smacking his forehead on a concrete floor. I asked a doctor at World Harvest Mission to examine him. He was given medication and asked to come back in a week. Upon returning to Cincinnati, I received an e-mail from Augustin. He wrote from an Internet café and was going to see the doctor the next day. "First of all, I want to thank you for your good friendship and your empathy," he said. "Because I was sick, you took good care of me. You treated me like your brother. You will be rewarded by the Almighty."

To this day, I can hardly read his words without tearing up. I don't know what to feel other than overwhelmed and unworthy. The more time I spend in Haiti, the less I understand it. The Haitian people humble me. Their spirit and faith inspire. They remind me that those of us with all in this world have a responsibility to those without, and to God. Much of the rest of organized religion feels increasingly like clutter, insulation to shield us from that obligation.

Such indomitable spirit was shown by our tap-tap driver,

Mackenson, on the side of the road in St. Marc; I watched him squat like a baseball catcher over a mud puddle and work furiously to repair his broken wheel and axle. He and a friend, who rode with him in the pickup's passenger seat, used an old jack to lift the truck. He stored tools in a ripped plastic bag behind the driver's seat. He didn't want to lose the fare and the day's work. As I watched, I could tell he had made this fix before. Mackenson had work and was clinging tightly to it. An estimated ninety thousand jobs had been lost in Haiti because of the earthquake, according to a U.N. source quoted in the *Economic Times.*[2]

The broken axle cost us forty-five minutes. I wasn't surprised we had run into trouble. Life in Haiti is a prime example of the adage about testing God's sense of humor by making plans. Then, less than an hour up the road, in the village of Estère, we would make a wrong turn, heading northwest instead of northeast. Almost another hour had passed before Augustin tapped on the window to stop the driver. Already late, we would completely miss our appointment at Hôpital Albert Schweitzer if we continued north to Gonaïves. The driver was confused. He thought we were supposed to go first to Gonaïves and then to the hospital.

Earlier, Augustin had called Louisilia Louis in Gonaïves and told her we were going to visit. (To my surprise, Augustin had a cell phone number for her.) She would tell the other two families. I badly wanted to see them. Now, though, sitting on the side of the road in the back of a tap-tap, surrounded by a barren, hard land, I said we had to turn around and drive to the hospital. I asked Augustin to call Louisilia and apologize. The narrow window to get to Gonaïves had slammed shut. I carried paper copies of three photographs of members of Louisilia's family that I needed to identify. Yet I had to complete my newspaper work. That obligation was first. June 29,

2008, would indeed remain my last day in Gonaïves—at least for the time being.

I asked Augustin to find out from Louisilia how her family and the others were faring. Was everyone still alive and relatively well? Had Fritz returned from overseas to his family? How had the earthquake affected their lives?

No one had died. No one was especially sick, other than normal ailments. Fritz had come back to his wife and children, Louisilia told Augustin. "Life is more difficult," Augustin told me after he hung up. "Everything is more expensive since the earthquake. Food is more expensive." One can of rice had gone from seventeen Haitian dollars to twenty-six dollars—roughly the same increase the people at Ebenezer Orphanage would tell me that night.

We drove back to the south, toward the turn we had missed. I fumed inside. I grew silent and stared out the slats of the tap-tap's wood frame. I clenched my jaw tight and grinded my teeth. We were just an hour from Gonaïves— a damn hour. I felt sorry for myself. I'd come all this way. I'd endured discomfort. I'd risked my health. I wasn't asking for much. Yet as I slid toward self-pity, I caught myself. Or God caught me. I thought of the Bible passage that had been read at breakfast the previous morning in Montrouis by Larry Bergeron, a former minister from Cincinnati whom I'd befriended. Bergeron had walked away from a high-paying corporate job on the East Coast and then a lucrative megachurch pulpit in suburban Cincinnati to start the nonprofit A Child's Hope International. Now he and his team had traveled to Haiti to give out food, but a Florida-based shipping company had failed to get the container holding 300,000 meals to Haiti for distribution.

Bergeron was frustrated and upset. "There are starving children everywhere," he said between cell phone calls.

"I have to do something." He tried to find food that A Child's Hope already had shipped to Haiti. If any was available in storage, could he borrow it? He would find seventy-five boxes at a ministry compound south of Montrouis. Bergeron would get the food to the Ebenezer Orphanage.

That Saturday, February 27—the day before my failed effort to get to Gonaïves and the day after his discovery that his food remained in Florida—Bergeron read aloud from Psalm 39: "Show me, O Lord, my life's end. And the number of my days; let me know how fleeting is my life." Bergeron said he didn't want to waste his time consumed by anger and frustration.

Now it was my turn to apply the teaching. Sitting in the back of the tap-tap—staring out at the expanse of deforested Haiti, broken up by a hut or a cinder-block wall, and then the rice fields of the Artibonite Valley—I could relate to Bergeron's situation. I decided to give up my anger, too. Yield to Haiti. I had tried to get to Gonaïves, yet it did not happen. Had my time in Haiti not taught me anything? I was not in control. There's a reason the word patience—*pasyans*—is emblazoned on brightly painted tap-taps and rickety old school buses; they always break down, forcing passengers to the side of the road to wait for repairs. One must have great patience to live day to day.

There's a proverb for just about everything in Haiti:

Pasyans bel, lavi long.
Beautiful patience, long life.

Instead of sulking, I decided to look for other opportunities to experience the land and people on that Sunday afternoon. So I immersed myself in that moment and in the moments that would come the rest of the day, and for the rest of the time in Haiti, giving them my complete attention—forgetting what wasn't there and what would not be. I was not going to Gonaïves. I would not see Fritz and Rosemène, Johnny and Edele, Louisilia, or their children—not on this trip. But I would come back again. I knew that now. I would visit them as I would any friend in the United States, staying in their home and living as they do.

The interviews and tour at Hôpital Albert Schweitzer were educational. The message: work with Haitians; don't try to fix their country for them, but stay engaged over time. We stopped at a rice field north of the village of Estère and talked to women preparing the grain for sale by pushing it with broomlike rakes to dry it on smooth, poured concrete slabs. The homegrown yellow rice was preferred by Haitians but more expensive than imported white rice. In the town of Atpotri, we spoke with an eighteen-year-old woman, Scheiline Petithome, who pumped water from a community well into white paint buckets and whose countenance and words—like those of many women in Haiti—dispensed wisdom well beyond her years and level of formal education. The water was cold and clear just like water from outdoor pumps I'd drunk in the United States. Yet it was nothing like it, teeming with bacteria that cause diseases such as typhoid fever, diarrhea, and dysentery and contribute to half of all deaths in Haiti. "We have no choice. It is the only water we have. Of course, it makes people sick," Scheiline told us.

Her comments would take on a dire dimension a few months later. A cholera outbreak—the first in Haiti in more than a century—started in October 2010, causing more than two thousand deaths and making another 91,700 sick nationwide through the first week of December. Violence broke out when a rumor spread, and was essentially verified by the U.S. Centers for Disease Control and Prevention (CDC), that the cholera bacteria originated with U.N. peacekeepers from Nepal in a camp outside the town of Mirebalais.[3] The strain matched one in South Asia. Human waste leaked from the military base into a tributary of the Artibonite River. The death rate in the first six weeks was 19 per 100,000 people, according to the CDC.[4] UNICEF officials expected the toll to go higher. About 1.5 million people, they estimated, live in conditions in Haiti that make them vulnerable to the spread of the waterborne disease, an infection of the small intestine that causes profuse watery diarrhea and vomiting.[5] Deaths occurred within two hours of a patient falling ill, some losing as much as one liter of fluid within the first hour.

In early November, the nation was spared another great loss of life when low-lying areas along the sea were evacuated ahead of Hurricane Tomas. Still, at least seven people died, and the heavy rain and runoff exacerbated the mounting health crisis. "We can use some help rebuilding a few school walls that were washed away, and with a water purification effort under way in the villages where cholera is spreading rapidly," the Reverend Gérard Dormévil told the U.S.-based development group Hands Together in an early November phone call from Gonaïves. Then the disputed results of the Haitian general election, which had been rescheduled from February 28 to November 28, triggered more violence that hampered—at least for a short time—international efforts to contain the spreading cholera epidemic.

Since I met the Cénécharles, Henrisma, and Louis families in May 2006, they have experienced two nationwide episodes of violent protests (caused by the 2010 election results and 2008 food shortages), four hurricanes and related flooding, a catastrophic earthquake, and a cholera epidemic. I repeatedly find myself wanting to contact them to ask whether they've survived another calamity. Selfishly, I also lamented that I couldn't hop on a plane, call, or send a fax to Gona-ïves to complete photo captions or clarify information. This assignment wasn't the typical newspaper story that allows for double- and triple-checking with the help of a public-relations staff. Even if I'd miraculously gotten through to Gonaïves, I couldn't justify asking people living on the edge of survival to do me a favor. A couple of loose ends would have to remain.

Reaching Gonaïves, an arduous journey in the best of times, was made nearly impossible by the layered tragedies faced by the people who live there. The longer view of their daily lives these many months later reinforced the lesson I came to understand while riding around the Artibonite Valley in a tap-tap on February 28, 2010.

I had plenty of safe water to drink.

I had a dinner of rice with chicken and fried plantains waiting that night.

I had medicine in my suitcase in case I became ill.

I had a job, one that actually meant something to me.

I had learned that the people I knew and cared for in Gonaïves were safe. And despite the widespread devastation in Port-au-Prince, Augustin and his wife and their five children and Father Tom of Hands Together were all safe too.

How did I want to live the rest of my fleeting days?

Appendix 1

Natural Disasters in Haiti

Even before the 7.3-magnitude earthquake of January 12, 2010, Haiti had a history of natural disasters in the past century, many worsened because 99 percent of its land is deforested and prone to erosion and flooding. Earthquakes and hurricanes have exacted a heavy toll on the small Caribbean nation. Concrete buildings are constructed, in part, to withstand hurricane winds and rain but are especially susceptible to earthquakes.

2010   A high-magnitude earthquake, centered just to the west of downtown Port-au-Prince, shook the capital during the late afternoon on January 12 and caused 230,000 deaths and widespread damage to an estimated 70 percent of the city's buildings.

2008   Three separate hurricanes—Gustav, Hanna, and Ike—and Tropical Storm Fay hit the country in a span of one month and accounted for eight hundred deaths, more than three hundred in the Gonaïves area. The city was under water, and more than half of the nation's crops were destroyed. Damage was estimated at one billion U.S. dollars.

2007   Tropical Storm Noel caused mudslides and floods that killed fifty-seven people.

2004 Hurricane Jeanne caused widespread flooding and landslides, and more than two thousand of its three thousand Haitian victims were killed in the Gonaïves area.

1998 Hurricane George caused more than four hundred deaths and destroyed 80 percent of the harvest.

1994 Hurricane Gordon accounted for the deaths of more than one thousand Haitians.

1963 Hurricane Flora's death toll in excess of six thousand people made it one of the deadliest Atlantic hurricanes recorded.

1954 Hurricane Hazel's death toll of one hundred people was relatively light, but one hundred towns were destroyed, and it ravaged about half of Haiti's coffee trees and cacao crop.

1946 The epicenter of an 8.1-magnitude earthquake, the largest recorded on the island of Hispaniola, was in the Dominican Republic and extended into Haiti. The quake and resulting tsunami killed almost 1,800 people.

1935 Two thousand people died in an unnamed storm.

1842 An earthquake destroyed Cap-Haïtien and other northern cities in Haiti and the Dominican Republic.

Source: Associated Press, "Timeline of Haiti's Natural Disasters," ABC News, January 13, 2010, *abcnews.go.com/International/ wireStory?id=9554940.*

Appendix 2

The Families

Henrisma Household

Dieudonné "Johnny" Henrisma: born 1961, unemployed
    mason, father of five children, two deceased
Edele Henrisma: born 1968, Johnny's wife
Dieunel: son, born 1990
Vava: daughter, born 1992 (living in countryside outside
    Gonaïves with her paternal grandmother)
Petyel: son, born 1993 (living in countryside outside
    Gonaïves with his paternal grandmother)
Nelson: son, born 1995
Denis: son, born 1998 (died at six months of age)
Luna: daughter, born 2000 (died at ten months of age)
Dieuna: daughter, born 2000

Cénécharles Household

Fritz Cénécharles: born 1963, unemployed mason, father of
    five children, has gone overseas to try to find work three
    times
Rosemène Cénécharles: born 1966, operates shop in main
    Gonaïves market selling household items and clothing
Mackenson: son, born 1987
Nadège: daughter, born 1989
Fritzlande: daughter, born 1991

Rosena: daughter, born 1993
Wisly: son, born 1999

Louis Household
Louisilia Louis: born 1966, widow, unemployed, mother of
   five children
Jean-Claude Cénécharles: died 2002, former husband of
   Louisilia
Prévilus Tony Cémouin: son, born 1990
Ketia Brunel: daughter, born 1992
Marqlyn Cénécharles: son, born 1997
Ronaldo Cénécharles: son, born 1999
Dgimy Cénécharles: son, born 2000
Oril Louis: born 1969, brother of Louisilia, widower, father of
   Micheline, born 2004
Dieumène Louis: born 1958, sister of Louisilia, widow,
   mother of three children, grandmother of one
Rosita Jacques: daughter, born 1981
Yvonia Prévilus: daughter, born 1985
Denise Prévilus: daughter, born 1988, and mother of
   Casonley Lerne, born 2003

Notes

Introduction
1. U.N. Children's Fund, "The State of the World's Children" (2007), *data.un.org/Data.aspx?q=haiti+orphans&d=SOWC&f= inID%3a88%3bcrID%3a153.*
2. Ibid.

Chapter 2
1. Tom Avril, "Years Later, City's Ash Is Dumped," *Philadelphia Inquirer*, August 10, 2002.
2. Bruce E. Beans, "The Waste That Didn't Make Haste: After a 16-Year, Five-Continent Odyssey, Incinerator Ash Returns Home to Pa.," *Washington Post*, July 17, 2002.
3. John Donnelly and Harold Maass, "Thousands of Fearful Haitians in Hiding after Massacre, Slums Ghostly," *Miami Herald*, April 27, 1994.
4. "Haitian Massacre Reported; Witnesses Say Soldiers Raided Pro-Aristide Slum," *Chicago Tribune*, April 26, 1994.
5. Alfonso Chardy, "Former Officers Are Sent Back to Haiti; They Face Prison for Role in Killings," *Miami Herald*, January 28, 2003.
6. Center for Justice and Accountability, San Francisco (2008), *www.cja.org/article.php?list=type&type=78.*
7. Gary Marx, "Haitians Flee Unrest in Port City; Violence Spreads to about 10 Towns," *Chicago Tribune*, February 10, 2004.
8. M. E. Beatty, E. Hunsperger, E. Long, J. Schurch, S. Jain, R. Colindres, et al., "Mosquitoborne Infections after Hurricane Jeanne, Haiti," U.S. Centers for Disease Control and Prevention, *Emerging Infectious Diseases Journal*, February 2007.

9. Reed Lindsay, "After Hurricane Ike, Haiti Copes with Aid Delays," *Christian Science Monitor*, September 15.

Chapter 3

1. United Nations, Department of Economic and Social Affairs, Population Division, "World Population Prospects: The 2008 Revision" (2009), *unstats.un.org/unsd/demographic/products/socind/health.htm*.

Chapter 4

1. World Health Organization, "Global Health Observatory" (2008).
2. U.S. Department of State, "2006 Country Reports on Human Rights Practices," *www.state.gov/g/drl/rls/hrrpt/2006/78895.htm*.

Chapter 6

1. U.N. Children's Fund, "The State of the World's Children" (2007), *data.un.org/Data.aspx?q=haiti+orphans&d=SOWC&f=inID%3a88%3bcrID%3a153*.
2. UNICEF, "Statistical Portrait of Haiti, 2007," *www.unicef.org/infobycountry/haiti_statistics.html*.
3. U.S. Central Intelligence Agency (CIA), "The World Fact Book" (2010), *www.cia.gov/library/publications/the-world-factbook/geos/ha.html*.

Chapter 7

1. BBC Monitoring International Reports and Caribbean Media Corporation, "Haitians Visiting Bahamas for Employment," September 20, 2006.
2. Dana Harmon, "Haitian Migrants Face Rising Backlash Next Door," *Christian Science Monitor*, January 24, 2006.
3. Ibid.
4. U.S. Department of State, "2006 Country Reports on Human Rights Practices," *www.state.gov/g/drl/rls/hrrpt/2006/78895.htm*.

Chapter 8

1. U.N. Statistics Division, "Social Indicators" (2010), *unstats.un.org/unsd/demographic/products/socind/inc-eco.htm*.

2. U.S. Agency for International Development, "Haiti," *www.usaid.gov/locations/latin_america_caribbean/country/haiti/*.

Chapter 12

1. Marianne Lavelle and Kent Garber, "Fixing the Food Crisis: There Are as Many Potential Solutions to the Price Hikes as Causes of Them, and None of Them Will Come Easily," *U.S. News and World Report*, May 19, 2008, 36–42.
2. Ibid.

Afterword

1. Oren Dorell, "Crews Begin to Raze Haiti's Hotel Montana," *USA Today*, January 28, 2010, *www.usatoday.com/news/world/2010-01-28-haiti-montana_N.htm*.
2. "90,000 Jobs Lost in Quake-Hit Haiti, UN Agency," *Economic Times*, March 5, 2010, *economictimes.indiatimes.com/news/news-by-industry/jobs/90000-jobs-lost-in-quake-hit-Haiti-UN-agency/articleshow/5647762.cms*.
3. Rong-Gong Lin II, "Cholera Now Throughout Haiti, U.S. Says," *Los Angeles Times*, December 9, 2010, *www.latimes.com/news/nation-world/world/la-fg-haiti-cholera-20101209,0,3947207.story*.
4. Rong-Gong Lin II, "Cholera in Haiti has spread to every part of the country, CDC reports," *Los Angeles Times*, December 8, 2010, *www.latimes.com/health/boostershots/la-heb-cholera-haiti-20101208,0,4182902.story*.
5. UNICEF, U.S. Fund, "Clean Water Campaign," *www.unicefusa.org/work/water/*.

Bibliography

Agee, James, and Walker Evans. *Let Us Now Praise Famous Men: Three Tenant Families.* New York: Houghton Mifflin, 1941; repr., 1988.

Cadet, Jean-Robert. *Restavec: From Haitian Slave to Middle-Class American.* Austin: University of Texas Press, 1998.

Curtis, James. *Mind's Eye, Mind's Truth: FSA Photography Reconsidered.* Philadelphia: Temple University Press, 1989.

Hersey, John. "Agee: Introduction," from *Let Us Now Praise Famous Men: Three Tenant Families.* New York: Houghton Mifflin, 1988.

Innocent, Claude. "The Poor Man's Life." In *Open Gate: An Anthology of Haitian Creole Poetry,* edited by Paul Laraque and Jack Hirschman. Willimantic, CT: Curbstone Press, 2001.

John Paul II. *The Gospel of Life: On the Value and Inviolability of Human Life.* Washington, DC: U.S. Conference of Catholic Bishops, 1995.

Kotlowitz, Alex. *The Other Side of the River.* New York: Doubleday, 1998.

Mapou, Jan. "Women of My Country." In *Open Gate: An Anthology of Haitian Creole Poetry,* edited by Paul Laraque and Jack Hirschman. Willimantic, CT: Curbstone Press, 2001.

Merton, Thomas. *Seeds of Contemplation.* New York: New Directions, 1949.

Métraux, Alfred. *Voodoo in Haiti.* New York: Schocken Books, 1972.

Mohanty, Chandra Talpade, Ann Russo, and Lourdes Torres, eds. *Third World Women and the Politics of Feminism.* Bloomington: Indiana University Press, 1991.

Morris, Errol. "The Case of the Inappropriate Alarm Clock." Seven-part series. *New York Times,* 2009, *opinionator.blogs.nytimes.com/category/the-case-of-the-inappropriate-alarm-clock/.*

Walker, Alice. *In Search of Our Mothers' Gardens.* New York: Harcourt, Brace, Jovanovich, 1983.

Index

199

Index

Trou Sable (neighborhood), 24, 27,
45–56, 73, 75–84, 98, 129–38, 142–
45, 167, **I-1**

unemployment rates, 27, 93, 95, 100,
109
uniforms, school, 3, 105, 115, 179, **II-8**
United Nations (U.N.)
and disaster relief, 2, 10, 42
as information source, 7, 55, 85,
108, 182
media office of, 181
U.N. peacekeepers, 186
U.S. Agency for International Development, 109
U.S. Department of Agriculture, 35–36
U.S. Environmental Protection Agency,
35–36
U.S. Mortuary Service, 176

Valmond, Herbert, 38
vendors, 56, 113, 132, 142–44, 172,
I-2. *See also* Cénécharles market
stand
Vincenzina, Sister, 110–11
violence, causes of
cholera outbreak, 185–86
gangs, 39, 102, 159
hunger, 42, 44, 138, 139–40
politics, 36–40, 186
voodoo, 135–37
Voodoo in Haiti (Métraux), 135

Walker, Alice, 59
waste, 1, 34, 37, 42, 51, 81, 118, 165,
186. *See also* plumbing, lack of
water
author's gratitude for, 166, 187
for construction, 80

for cooking, 81, 144–45
coordinator of, 172
diseases borne by, 30–31, 185–86
and hospitality, 11, 30–31, 125
and hunger, 142
for irrigation, 40, 178
shortage of, 1, 9, 42, 96, 141, 157
in streets, 46, 47, 114, 137, 142
transport of: in paint buckets, 28,
81, 82, 116, 117, 144, 185; in
pouches, 30, 113–14; by pump,
40, 144; by slave children, 61
treatment of, 175, 186
for washing, 30, 81, 117, 121, 147
and waste disposal, 34, 81, 118,
186
wells as supply of, 80, 81, 82, 97,
116, 147, 185
See also rain
wealth, and Haitian elite, 50, 87, 109,
168
western hemisphere, Haiti's status in,
87, 100, 106, 108, 152
West Nile virus, 43
"Whatsoever You Do" (hymn), 164
whites
blan as term for, 49, 123
children's reactions to, 21, 29, 174
and exploitation of Haitians, 86–88
expulsion from Haiti, 135
guilt of, 86, 137
images of, 15, 79
neighbors' reactions to, 113, 114
See also *blan* (white), author
addressed as
womanists, 59
"Women of My Country" (Mapou), 58
World Harvest Mission, 175, 181
World Health Organization, 58